What Daughters Are Saying About *Embracing Your Father*

"Before reading this book I only thought about how my father affected my life—never about how I affected his life. Finally I am able to see him as a person with his own life, his own dreams, his own fears."

"I couldn't imagine ever talking to my father about feelings. But when I started asking him Nielsen's questions about his childhood, he was fighting to hold back tears. I actually reached over to him and said it was okay to talk to me about his father. It was a first—me reaching out to comfort my dad."

"Even though I am a wife and mother, I was still hiding certain things from my father because I wanted him to think of me as this perfect, innocent little girl. Since I've been more open and honest with him, we're finally relating like two adults."

"I have stopped running to my mother when I'm upset with my father. I go directly to him. And that has made all the difference. He even told me how it had always hurt him when I went through mom to communicate with him."

"Because I have changed the way I interact with my father, I finally realize that we have both been wanting the same thing from our relationship all these years. We just never talked enough to figure that out."

"I could never imagine having conversations with my father about anything personal. But now I'm relating to him personally as someone other than an extension of my mother."

"The mere mention of my father used to bring me to tears. I envied other daughters. And I never expected to be shown a way to remedy this ache. We have reconnected."

"It has been so moving to hear my father say that the most loving gift I have ever given him is deciding finally that I want to get to know him."

Embracing
Your Father

Embracing
Your Father
How to Build
the Relationship
You've Always Wanted
with Your Dad

Linda Nielsen

McGRAW-HILL

New York Chicago San Francisco Lisbon
London Madrid Mexico City Milan New Delhi
San Juan Seoul Singapore Sydney Toronto

1 2 3 4 5 6 7 8 9 0 DOC/DOC 0 9 8 7 6 5 4

ISBN 0-07-142303-6

This publication is designed to provide accurate and authoritative information in regard to the subject matter covered. It is sold with the understanding that the publisher is not engaged in rendering legal, accounting, or other professional service. If legal advice or other expert assistance is required, the services of a competent professional person should be sought.

> —*From a declaration of principles jointly adopted by a committee of the American Bar Association and a committee of publishers.*

McGraw-Hill books are available at special quantity discounts to use as premiums and sales promotions, or for use in corporate training programs. For more information, please write to the Director of Special Sales, Professional Publishing, McGraw-Hill, Two Penn Plaza, New York, NY 10121-2298. Or contact your local bookstore.

 This book is printed on recycled, acid-free paper containing a minimum of 50% recycled, de-inked fiber.

Library of Congress Cataloging-in-Publication Data

Nielsen, Linda.
  Embracing your father : how to build the relationship you always wanted with your dad / Linda Nielsen.— 1st ed.
    p. cm.
  Includes bibliographical references.
  ISBN 0-07-142303-6 (hardcover : alk. paper)
  1. Fathers and daughters. 2. Parent and child. 3. Interpersonal relations. 4. Interpersonal communication. I. Title.
  HQ755.85.N528 2004
  306.874'2—dc22

                                                        2004000789

In memory of my father,
Nils Nielsen.

Contents

Acknowledgments

First and foremost, I am indebted to the daughters and fathers who have shared their personal experiences with me and allowed me to help them explore their relationships. Without their candor, their trust, and their dedication to father-daughter relationships, this book would not have come into being. A special thanks to Randy Nance in this regard.

I am fortunate to have compassionate friends who have supported my work by easing my emotional, physical, and professional pains along the way: Debbie Cooper, Jeni Geisler, Mary DeShazer, Anne Dickason, Leo Duffer, Tina Shipp, and Ulrike Wiethaus. Without your support after Zoe died, I could not have finished the book.

Many thanks to my agent, Jim Levine, whose advice was immensely helpful from beginning to end, and to his assistant, Meylinda Bissmeyer, whose attentiveness was always reassuring. I appreciate the talented people at McGraw-Hill who shepherded the book through to completion: my editor Nancy Hancock, her assistant Meg Leder, editing supervisor Pattie Amoroso, and copyeditor Jim Madru.

Finally, I am grateful to my mother, Frances Nielsen, for sharing her feelings and experiences with me in ways that have allowed me to explore my relationship with my father more fully. And no one has given me as much insightful feedback, comfort, and encouragement as my beloved husband, Steve Mizel. He not only came up with the title for the book, but invested more hours than anyone discussing and helping me refine my ideas.

Introduction

- Are you having trouble communicating with your father?

- Have you been out of touch with you father for years and are wondering how to reconnect with him?

- Do you wonder if it's worth trying to improve your relationship with your father?

- Do you ever envy other daughters' relationships with their fathers?

- Are there certain things you'd really like to talk with your father about, but you're too afraid?

- Do you feel that your relationship with your father isn't very good, but you can't figure out why?

- Has your parents' divorce complicated your relationship with your father?

- Do you end up feeling tense, annoyed, or angry when you're with your father?

- Do you pretend to be someone you're not when you're with your father?

- Do you wish that you were more relaxed and open with each other?

- Do you feel your father loves one of your siblings more than he loves you?

- Do you think that your father is too demanding, too critical, or too bossy?

- Have financial issues created bad feelings between you?

- Is it hard for you to argue or to disagree with your father?

- Do you find it difficult to forgive or apologize to each other?

- Would you like to get closer to your father, but you're afraid that it might make your mother jealous?

- Do you ever feel that you're a disappointment to your father—or is he a disappointment to you?

- Do you think that your father cares too much about his work and not enough about you?

If you answered yes to any of these questions, keep reading because I wrote this book with you in mind. My goal is to teach you ways to embrace your father more fully. But what do I mean by *embrace*? To embrace can mean "to hug," but I'm referring to the deeper meanings of the word— accept, adopt, encompass, embody, encircle, choose, welcome, receive, incorporate, include, consider, believe in, open up to, allow in, hold dear, and love.

Embracing doesn't mean clinging or hanging onto someone like a dependent or desperate child. And it doesn't mean that you have to agree or get along all the time with the other person. But embracing does mean that you do not discard, ignore, push away, exclude, reject, or shun your father. *Embracing Your Father* means just what it says. In this book, *you are the adult who is going to* **do** *the embracing—not the little girl who is silently, angrily, sadly, or passively waiting for her father to embrace her.*

Why should you be the one to have to take the initiative? After all, no matter how old you are, your father is still your parent, and you are still his child. Isn't it his responsibility to have a good relationship with you? If you take the initiative, isn't that putting the blame on yourself, admitting the problem is your fault?

And you may be wondering, why should you listen to me? Let me give you some background that will help to answer these questions.

During the last 30 years, as a professor of psychology at Wake Forest University in Winston-Salem, North Carolina, I have been working with adolescent and young-adult daughters. For the past 10 years, I have been teaching the only course in the country devoted exclusively to father-daughter relationships. In a sense, my course is a legacy of my relationship with my own father. We had a rocky relationship during the 1960s, a time of political and social upheaval when I was coming of age. Even though my students have grown up in a different time, I repeatedly saw many of them struggling with the same father-daughter issues. After my father died, I created a course to help daughters strengthen their relationships with their fathers.

The results, I'm happy to say, have been nothing short of phenomenal. The techniques that I have developed for my course and used in workshops have helped hundreds of women strengthen or reestablish relationships with their fathers. Here is just a small sample of what daughters say after they have learned to take the initiative and embrace their fathers:

- "The mere mention of my father used to reduce me to tears. I never expected to be shown a way to remedy this ache. But now my dad and I are actually spending time together."

- "If it weren't for Dr. Nielsen's work, I still wouldn't be speaking to my dad after not talking to him for 8 years since my parents' divorce."

- "I have really gotten to know my father as more than an extension of my mother."

- "Because of what I've learned from Dr. Nielsen, it's hard for me to be angry with dad anymore."

- "Talking to my dad about my mother's death had always been taboo until I followed the advice in this book."

- "Dr. Nielsen helped me jump-start the process of fixing my relationship with my dad."

- "I could never imagine having a conversation with my father about feelings. But now I see my dad as so much more than just my father."

In this book I'm going to share the techniques that have worked so effectively in helping other daughters embrace their fathers more fully. I'll help you to discover ways to share more of yourself with your father and get him to share more of himself with you. I have included the same quizzes and advice that have worked so well for my students. If you use them, they can open your eyes to things you've never considered before about you and your father. And no matter how old you are, you can learn new ways to strengthen your relationship with your father.

Why Should You Take the Initiative?

Almost every daughter feels that her father ought to be the one to go first. No matter how minor or major the need for a better relationship, he should take the first step to initiate contact, to try again, to ease tensions, to apologize, or to make a change for the sake of your relationship. After all, he is the parent and he is older than you, right? If this is how you feel, there are three beliefs that are probably holding you back.

Belief 1: The person who is older and therefore more mature, more established, more self-confident, or more powerful ought to be the initiator.

Contrary to popular belief, a well-established body of research on personality development, aging, and parenting has shown that growing older or being a success outside the family *does not* necessarily or automatically make adults more mature or more confident in their roles as parents.

As you read my book, you're going to discover many ways in which you are probably more mature, more confident, and more skilled than your father in those areas which have the greatest impact on your relationship. In fact, you're going to learn that if your father is like the vast majority of men in our country, he has not been given nearly as much training or as much opportunity as you have to learn how to communicate intimately or to initiate changes in close relationships. You're also going to learn that those men who have the most in terms of money, success, status, education, or power often have the least in terms of confidence and skill when it comes to knowing how to reach out or resolve problems with their daughters.

Look at it this way: If you and your father were stranded on a raft at sea, and if you had been trained in sea survival, would you be sulking or waiting for him to take the first step because he is older than you or because he is your parent? And what good would his wealth, his success, or his impressive degrees do the two of you if you were the only one who knew how to swim, how to row, or how to repair the leak in your boat? This may seem like a ridiculous comparison to you, but as you read my book you are going to discover that your father is often less equipped or less confident than you are when it comes to fixing the leaks in your relationship or steering your relationship back on the right course. In short, *if you believe that the person who is the most mature, most confident, or most skilled should go first, that person is often you, not your father.*

Belief 2: It is the parent's responsibility to take the lead and to work the hardest in relationships with their children.

Yes, it's true that when you were a child, your father had to assume 100 percent of the responsibility for your relationship. There was no other choice, given your physical, emotional, and mental immaturity. You were completely dependent on adults for your survival. And like all children, you were mainly focused on yourself—your feelings, your needs, and your problems. In a sense, you weren't capable of having a real relationship with a parent. Like all of us, as you were growing up, you were having to learn how to create relationships with other human beings—how to get beyond thinking only of yourself, how to see things from someone else's viewpoint, and how to give and take.

By the time you became a teenager, you were discovering that it takes two to tango. That is, you were learning that you have to do your share of the work and the initiating if you want to have satisfying relationships. Above all, you were learning that sometimes you had to be the one to go first when it came to apologizing, forgiving, reaching out, trying to resolve problems, or giving it another try. With those friends you loved the most, you probably swallowed your pride many times and took the first step toward patching things up even when both of you knew that it was the other person's turn and even when you knew that the problem had been caused by something the other person did.

You probably sense where I'm headed with this. Why aren't you behaving the same way toward your father that you behave in your other relationships during difficult times? And why are you so wedded to the idea that *he* has to assume the initiative when you cut your other friends more slack? Odds are that the answer is this: You haven't moved beyond seeing yourself as a little girl whose daddy is supposed to take full responsibility for your relationship. Even at your age, maybe you haven't gotten to the point where you are willing to assume equal initiative and equal responsibility for your relationship with your father—which means that sometimes you will have to do more than your fair share of the work, just like you do in many of your other relationships.

Don't get me wrong. I am *not* suggesting that you should do most of the work or most of the initiating on a regular basis with your father—or with anyone else for that matter. But there are times in any relationship where one person has to do most of the giving and most of the initiating. *You have just as much responsibility as your father to take the first step or try again—and yes, there are times when you will end up doing more than he.*

Belief 3: The person who has put the least into the relationship or done the most damage should make the first move.

If you generally sit back waiting for the person who did the most damage or put the least into a relationship to take the initiative, to apologize, or to take the first step toward setting things straight again, you probably spend a lot of time being disappointed and angry.

Let's leave your father aside for a minute. Think back to those times when you have hurt someone you loved or made big mistakes in your relationship—*really big ones.* What do you usually do? Do you sometimes feel so ashamed, embarrassed, awkward, or guilty that you honestly don't know what to do next, so you do nothing at all? Do you ever let months or maybe even years go by without addressing the issue head on? Do you ever pretend that it never happened and try to avoid ever bringing it up again? Do you fear contacting that person again or asking for a second chance? Do you think that you've screwed up so badly that there is no way to make things right again? Do you ever feel relieved when the injured party eventually makes the first move? I'm sure you get my point: *The person who has damaged or limited a relationship the most often has the harder time reaching out, apologizing, or trying to set things right again.*

Why Try Again? What's in It for You?

If you've repeatedly tried to improve your relationship with your father, but nothing seems to change, you're probably not going to be very interested in trying the suggestions in my book, are you? But you've read this far and you picked this book up for some reason—either because you do still have some hope or because someone you respect has asked you to read this because they still have hope. If you're wondering whether to try again, you're probably telling yourself: He's never going to change. I'm never going to change. And at my age it doesn't much matter what kind of relationship he and I have or I'll only end up more hurt, angry, or frustrated than I already am.

Before we talk about your father, I'd like you to think about some other relationship in your life that went through rough times or maybe even ended altogether for a period of time but then got better. Before things started improving or before you got back together again, didn't you sometimes feel that neither of you would change, the relationship wasn't worth the trouble any more, and there was nothing more in it for you? Don't most of us feel pessimistic and powerless when things aren't going well or have hit rock bottom in a relationship? But if we have any interest left in a relationship at all, we try again. We plunge ahead—or maybe we just bumble slowly along. But we usually try to learn from our mistakes and give it another go. This reminds me of something that Thomas Edison supposedly said to a young coworker who had lost hope. "Mr. Edison," said the discouraged worker, "I'm sorry to report that we have done 1000 experiments and worked thousands of hours on this, but it has all been for nothing." "Nonsense!" Edison replied, "We have had the good fortune of learning 1000 ways in which it does not work."

As for you and your father, the question is: Are you going to give your pessimistic, helpless thoughts power over you—or are you going to try again? You're probably only willing to say yes if you have some reason to believe that it might turn out better this time, if you truly believe that there is something in it for you, or if you believe that you won't end up more hurt, angry, or frustrated than you are now. And that's what I'll be trying to get you to see throughout this book. For now, I'd like you to consider what you might have in common with the following three thirsty daughters.

The first daughter is literally dying of thirst. But she's in luck—she finds a well. Of course, the water is too far down the well for her to reach with her hand. Luck again—next to the well is a bucket, a rope, and a hammer. She picks up the hammer, ties it to the rope, and tries lifting drops of water on the hammer's head. She tries again and again and again. Eventually, she dies of thirst. Like this daughter, maybe you keep picking up the wrong tools when you're trying to quench your thirst for a better relationship with your father. I'm going to be offering you some new tools—new ways to embrace your father. Again, if you think back to other relationships in your life that improved or blossomed again after you had almost given up hope, I'll bet things didn't improve until one of you started using some different approaches—put down the hammer, pick up the bucket. *Maybe you haven't been using the right approaches with your father.*

Or are you more like the second thirsty daughter? She isn't dying of thirst, but she's had a throbbing headache all day because she's so dehydrated. She sees the well. She knows not to use that hammer to get what she wants. But she feels that it's just too inconvenient in this heat to hook the bucket to the rope and haul up the cool water. She is also afraid to get too close to the well because she almost fell down a well when she was a little girl. She'd rather put up with her headache than approach that deep, dark, scary well. Of course, what she'd really like is for someone to come along and haul the water out for her. But because she doesn't need the water to survive, and because she has gotten used to having so many headaches like this over the years, she decides to walk on by the well—head throbbing. Like her, you may be a relatively happy person who truly doesn't *need* a better relationship with your father. You're getting along just fine with things the way they are now, despite the continued aches and pains of your relationship with your father. You two somehow manage to get along. But what about the jealousy you feel when you hear other daughters talk about their wonderful relationships with their fathers? Or what about those sad feelings you get when you watch a tender movie about a father and daughter? What I'm saying is this: *No matter how old you are, a better relationship with your father has benefits for you, even if you are relatively happy with other parts of your life.*

Maybe you're more like the third thirsty daughter. She and her father are both dying of thirst. Both know they need the rope and bucket to get water from the well. Unfortunately, the two of them have been seriously injured and can't bend their elbows. They can still use their hands to haul the water up, which they do. But the way the water bucket is designed, a person can't bend far enough into it to get any water. So the bucket of water sits on the ground between the thirsty father and daughter. How can they save themselves? Answer: If they will each lift the bucket up with their unbending arms and tilt it toward the other's mouth, they can both drink to their hearts' content. *If you are willing to try a different approach and to work with what you have—your imperfections and his—you may quench your thirst for a better relationship with your father.*

Having said all this, I'm convinced that the biggest payoff for you is how you feel about yourself. Assuming the very worst, let's say that your pessimistic assumptions turn out to be right: No matter how many of my suggestions you try or how many more times you try, your relationship with your father doesn't get any better. Yes, you'll be disappointed, frustrated, and sad—and maybe angry. But these are the same feelings you had before you started. So you really haven't lost anything. And I seriously doubt that you're going to regret having tried. Every daughter I know who has reached out and tried again, regardless of the outcome, feels better about herself. It's as if she has lifted a weight off her shoulders. Like these daughters, you can give yourself the gift of pride and respect that comes from being active instead of passive, from acting like an adult instead of a child, and from being more loving and less rejecting. *By trying again to embrace your father, you embrace the best of yourself.*

This Is the Book for You if . . .

You want to make some changes in the way you relate to your father. There's an old joke among therapists: How many psychologists does it take to change a light bulb? Only one, *but the light bulb has to want to be changed.* I don't have the power to make you *want* to change the way you relate to your father. Nobody does except you. Since you're not a light bulb, you can't be changed by any psychologist. Change is something you have to do yourself. But what I *can* change for you is this: I can change your being uninformed about ways to behave differently around your dad. I can give you information and tactics that have worked for other daughters to improve their relationships with their fathers.

You want to focus more on improving your relationship than on blaming people—including yourself—for their mistakes and shortcomings. This book is not focused on blaming people for their imperfections.

Instead, I'm inviting you to focus on things you can do to enhance your relationship with your father. I'm certain that both you and your father have blamed each other at times for things that were, in fact, not the other person's fault. So, as you read, keep this in mind: Nature didn't make any of us perfect, so it did the next best thing by making all of us blind to our own faults.

You are willing to consider what research and the experiences of other daughters and fathers have to offer, even though they may differ from your own personal experiences. I'm going to be giving you information in boxes I call "Eye Openers." These brief summaries of research and statistics are intended to make you think a little differently about you and your father. Many of these "Eye Openers" will surprise you. Others will anger you. Still others may sadden or unsettle you. That's okay. All I'm asking is that when the information differs from your own experience or your own beliefs, try to keep an open mind. There's a tendency in all of us to ignore or argue with any information that makes us question our own beliefs or our own behavior. Just remember: Minds, like parachutes, function best when open.

You are willing to do some things that might make you uncomfortable at first. If you're willing to step outside your comfort zone and do some things differently with your father, you will get the most out of this book. This means giving up your wishbone and developing more backbone. I can't guarantee that if you follow my advice you'll end up with an absolutely splendid father-daughter relationship. But I can guarantee you this: Wishing things would change is like waiting for Prince Charming or a magic frog to hop into your life to solve your problems. You have got to be willing to feel some discomfort in order to get what you want. And it's perfectly natural to feel nervous or uncomfortable. Here is what daughters generally say about leaving their comfort zones:

- "It wasn't easy at first, but now I'm glad that Dr. Nielsen asked us the hard personal questions that other people hesitate to ask."
- "I can't say that I liked her course in the beginning. In fact, I thought about dropping out. But she really got us to dig deep

into ourselves, to understand and accept the reasons why we and our fathers act the way we do."

- "I had to look at a lot of painful things that I' d been avoiding. But I'm so glad I did what she suggested."

- "She raised uncomfortable questions that made me think and opened my mind about my family."

- "She handled topics that you normally just don't discuss any-where else."

- "She tells us things we haven't heard before because no one else has been honest or candid enough to make us take off our rose-colored glasses like she does."

You are willing to look at your relationship from your father's point of view. There's a fable about a little girl who asks how Tarzan could have been so smart, so strong, so wonderful, and so wise to conquer and outsmart every single animal all by himself, frightening and defeat-ing even the mighty lions. The grown-up answers: "Child, if the lion ever learns to speak and write, you're going to hear a very different story." In the same way, I'm trying to get you to see the lion's side of father-daughter relationships—to consider the feelings and the expe-riences of fathers. Like the lions in the fable, most of our fathers have never gotten to tell their stories or to have their voices heard.

Are You Ready?

Many daughters tell me that they want a closer relationship with their father, but they say they "aren't ready yet" to start working on it. They have dozens of reasons why it's just "not the right time." What all these daugh-ters have in common is this: They believe that there is plenty of time left to work on their father-daughter relationship or to get to know their father better. If you feel this way, grab hold of this reality: Half of us will not have a father who is still alive by the time we reach age 50. Since the average woman lives to be 85, you have only a 50/50 chance that your father will be alive for any of the last 30 years of your life.

Seven Slippery Slopes

Over the past 30 years in my work as a psychologist and researcher, I have come to recognize the situations and the beliefs that generally make it more difficult for daughters to embrace their relationships with their fathers fully. I have categorized these situations into what I call the *seven slippery slopes:* (1) negative beliefs about fathers, (2) money and work, (3) communication, (4) getting to know each other, (5) mothers' feelings and behaviors, (6) sex and dating, and (7) parents' divorce and remarriage. When fathers and daughters get it right on these slippery slopes, they end up with a comfortable, loving, affirming relationship. When they get it wrong, though, they end up sliding down the slippery slope and ending up with a distant, strained, troubled relationship—or with no relationship at all. Most of us probably fall somewhere in between. We and our fathers do a great job getting up some of those slippery slopes, but we haven't gotten very far on others.

Will It Be Worth It?

If you decide to follow the advice I'm offering you in this book, will it be worth it? Will you actually notice any improvement in your relationship with your dad? To answer this, let me share a few more comments from those adult daughters who have attended my workshops over the past 10 years.

- "I feel embarrassed now realizing how hasty I was in judging my father and his motives."

- "I have stopped running to mommy like a little kid every time I'm upset with dad. I now talk directly to him."

- "I used to only think about my father in terms of me and how he affected my life. Now I think about how I affect him."

- "Talking about my mother's death has always been taboo, until I took this course."

- "By engaging in the activities in the book, my dad and I learned how to talk about some pretty painful issues."

- "I didn't think my dad and I had much to improve on. I was so wrong. I have started getting to know him as a person, and we're actually talking like two grown-ups."

I share these comments with you hoping that they will give you courage and energy to follow through on my advice. Although I don't know you or your father, I do know that some of what I'm going to suggest that you do or think about will be difficult for you. I sincerely hope and wholeheartedly believe that what I have written will lead you to deeper, more compassionate ways of *Embracing Your Father*.

Chapter 1

Expand Your Vision
Don't Be Blinded by Negative Beliefs

D o you believe that fathers

- Have less natural intuition for raising kids than mothers do?

- Get as much or more pleasure from their jobs than from their kids?

- Have much less impact on their daughters than mothers?

- Sacrifice less than mothers for their children?

- Are more critical and judgmental than mothers?

If you answered yes to many of these, your beliefs are blinding you to certain realities about fathers—including your own. Certain beliefs about men as parents make it harder for fathers and daughters to have as close a relationship as they might have otherwise. Our beliefs can be like blindfolds that prevent us from seeing our fathers clearly or from accepting more of what they have to offer us as parents. Our beliefs also influence what we remember and how we interpret our memories of our fathers. So the challenge is to figure out which of our beliefs and perceptions may be limiting or damaging our relationship. Let's start by looking at your family's beliefs. Then we'll see how your beliefs have influenced your perceptions of your father.

Your Family's Beliefs

In the chapters that follow we're going to look at hundreds of beliefs that may have limited your relationship with your father. For now, let's just consider

1

Your Family's Beliefs: Helping or Hurting?

When you were growing up, what did you and your parents believe? In addressing the following statements, use 0 for "strongly agree," 1 for "agree somewhat," and 2 for "strongly disagree."

Me Dad Mom

___ ___ ___ Fathers generally have less impact on their daughters than mothers do.

___ ___ ___ A daughter benefits more from a good relationship with her mother than with her father.

___ ___ ___ Mothers know more than fathers about what's good for kids.

___ ___ ___ Fathers lack the natural instincts that mothers have for raising children.

___ ___ ___ Mothers sacrifice more than fathers do for their children.

___ ___ ___ Daughters raised mainly by their mother are better adjusted and happier than those raised mainly by their father.

___ ___ ___ Fathers enjoy their jobs as much or more so than they enjoy their children.

___ ___ ___ Fathers are less interested than mothers in spending time with their daughters.

___ ___ ___ A daughter benefits most when her mother stays home and her father earns the family's income.

___ ___ ___ Mothers enjoy being parents more than fathers do, especially with daughters.

___ ___ ___ Scores (20 possible)

the 10 beliefs in this quiz to think back to what your family believed as you were growing up.

If every person in your family scored 20, you and your father probably have a communicative, comfortable, emotionally intimate relationship. Your family had the kinds of beliefs that generally create the best relationships between fathers and daughters. As you can see from the "Eye Openers" below, your family's beliefs also reflected the truth as best we know it from research and nationwide statistics. On the other hand, if your family's individual scores are lower than 10, you probably have a fairly uncomfortable, distant, or superficial relationship with your dad. You might get along fairly well, but you really don't know one another very well or spend much time together. This is mainly because your family put the greatest emphasis on your relationship with your mother and had some rather unflattering beliefs about men as parents.

So what? Why does it matter what your family believed about fathers as you were growing up? It matters because your family's beliefs have shaped how you and your family interacted with one another year after year. In turn, those interactions have shaped the kind of relationship you have with your dad. Think of yourselves like actors in a play. Your family's beliefs are the scripts. Your family's particular script tells each of you how you're supposed to act and what to expect from each other as you age. You each act out your roles in father-daughter, mother-daughter, and husband-wife pairings. I am not saying that there's no freedom in families to deviate from our scripts. I am saying, though, that long before you were born, your father's beliefs and your mother's beliefs about how fathers were supposed to act and what father-daughter relationships were supposed to be were creating the scripts that you and your father eventually would act out. Even as a very young child you were learning how you

Eye Openers

- Daughters raised mainly by their fathers are just as well adjusted and happy as daughters raised mainly by their mothers.[1,2]
- Women are *taught* how to be mothers, not born with maternal instincts that automatically make them better parents than men.[3–6]
- Most dads wish they could spend more time with their kids and less time at work.[7–9]
- Fathers and daughters are usually closer when the mother works full time outside the home while the children are growing up.[10–12]

and your father were supposed to interact and what kind of relationship you and he were supposed to have.

Let me give you an example of one very common belief that limits most father-daughter relationships. The belief goes something like this: Because the mother and daughter are both female, they "should" share more with each other and talk more comfortably about what's going on in their lives—especially personal things having to do with feelings and relationships. Because dad is a male, he isn't going to be very interested in, insightful about, or sensitive to those aspects of his daughter's life having to do with emotional stuff. Having picked up this belief from her parents at an early age, the daughter goes to her mother whenever she wants to talk about feelings, problems with friends, or matters of the heart such as love and dating. By the time she's a teenager, the daughter is convinced that "dad isn't interested in talking to me about emotional stuff. He's not sensitive or smart about that kind of thing. Talking like that would make both of us uncomfortable. We talk about the easy stuff like cars, grades, and sports." I can't tell you how many daughters have said this to me. Yet, when I ask them, "How often have you tried to talk to your dad about anything personal or emotional?" almost none of them have given their dad the opportunity to share this side of himself. In other words, the family's initial belief caused everyone to interact in ways that limited the father-daughter relationship.

Of course, not all families have the same beliefs about what father-daughter relationships should be. For instance, some families believe that fathers and daughters should talk just as openly and comfortably as mothers and daughters about personal, emotional, or sensitive topics. Unfortunately, though, many of our beliefs limit the kind of relationship a father and daughter can create together. So use the quiz on page 5 to find the connections between your family's beliefs and the kind of relationship you and your father have developed over the years.

If you scored higher than 20 on this quiz, you have given your father as much chance as you have given your mother to create an emotionally intimate, open, and comfortable relationship with you. But if you scored lower than 10, the way you treat your father probably has limited him to a fairly superficial, distant, or uncomfortable relationship with you. Now compare your score on this quiz with your score on the "Family Beliefs"

Have You Been Pushing Your Dad Away?

How have your beliefs about fathers and about father-daughter relationships affected the way you have treated your father over the years? In addressing the following statements, use 0 for "never," 1 for "rarely," and 2 for "half the time," and 3 for "almost always." Here's an example to get you started:

__1__ I tell my father as much about my personal life as I tell my mother.
My belief: Men aren't interested in personal or emotional things like women are.

____ I talk directly to my dad instead of going through my mother to communicate with him.
My belief:

____ I go to my father for advice and comfort about personal things.
My belief:

____ I ask my dad what's going on in his life besides his work.
My belief:

____ I tell my father as much about my day-to-day life as I tell my mother.
My belief:

____ I ask my father to do things alone with me so that we have time to talk privately.
My belief:

____ I have spent just as much time getting to know my father as I have with my mother.
My belief:

____ I encourage my dad to ask me questions about my life.
My belief:

____ I ask my dad about his life as a child and as a young man.
My belief:

____ My father and I spend time together without any other family members around.
My belief:

____ I am as open and honest with my dad as I am with my mom.
My belief:

____ Your score (30 possible)

quiz. Odds are the scores are similar. That is, the more positive beliefs you and your parents had about fathers and daughters while you were growing up, the more likely you are to have treated your father in ways that allowed him to develop an emotionally open and comfortable relationship with you.

Your Memories: Beware!

The beliefs you've grown up with also have shaped the way you perceive your father and what you do or do not remember about him. Your perception includes the way you interpret what he says and does, what you assume his motives are, and what meaning you give to his behavior. Your perceptions also influence and are influenced by your memories. And like your perceptions, your memories are based on what information your brain chooses to store or to ignore—and what meaning it gives to that information when you try to recall it later on.

The Greek philosopher Seneca wrote: "Your eyes will not see when your heart wishes them to be blind." In other words, our beliefs have the potential to blind us to reality by altering our perceptions about other people. Whether we're talking about fathers or used car dealers, our initial beliefs about other groups of people have a tremendous impact on what we notice and remember about them, how we interpret what they do, and how we behave around them. If our initial beliefs and expectations about a particular group are positive (grandmothers, little babies, or puppies), then our relationship with anyone in that group is off to a good start even before we meet them. We expect and predict good things from our relationships with them. But if our beliefs about a particular group are negative (stepmothers, used car dealers, or snakes), then our relationships start out with a handicap. We expect and predict bad things. We interpret what "they" do with a wary, negative, or suspicious eye. ("Watch out for snakes!" or "Beware of stepmothers!")

What you believe about men as parents can lead you to deceive yourself into assuming things about your dad that are not at all true or are only partially true. In fact, if every belief you have about fathers as a group were positive or flattering, you would still perceive your own dad inaccurately at times—but at least your misperceptions would be working in favor of your relationship. For example, if you were taught to believe that fathers were generally more nurturing than mothers, you would tend to perceive your dad and to interpret the things he did as being more nurturing than your mom. But as you'll see in later chapters (and as you probably already know from the quizzes you've taken so far in this chapter), a number of our beliefs about fathers are not very flattering—not nearly as flattering as our beliefs about mothers.[13,14]

So let's see what the researchers tell us about how our beliefs and expectations affect our relationships by influencing the way our brain processes information. (Since the group we're interested in is fathers, I've stated the research in terms of you and your dad.) *When you believe that something is generally true about fathers, even though the facts, the statistics, or the research do not support you, your belief still affects your relationship in these ways:*[15-18]

- You make assumptions about how your father is going to behave.

- You interpret his behavior to fit the beliefs and expectations you started with.

- You notice and exaggerate the things he does that fit your initial beliefs and expectations.

- You ignore or downplay the things he does that contradict your beliefs and expectations—even when he does something positive.

- You treat him in ways that make him more likely to behave the way you expect.

- You feel uncomfortable or confused when he does the opposite of what you expect.

- You're more likely to remember the things he does that fit your initial beliefs and expectations and to forget the things he does that contradict them.

All these things are going on while your brain collects, interprets, and stores incoming information about your father and about your relationship. Here's an overly simplified version of what happens. (Remember: Each of these three steps is affected by whatever beliefs and expectations you started out with.). First, your brain filters all incoming information and decides what to admit and what to ignore, what to remember and what to forget, and what to emphasize and what to downplay. Second, your brain interprets or gives meaning to whatever information it has allowed to enter. At this point you are judging your father's motives and his intensions. You are telling yourself either a positive or a negative story about the information your brain has allowed to enter. Remember, though, you have not allowed all the information to enter. Whatever good or bad story you are creating about your dad is based on partial and sometimes faulty data. Third, depending on the kind of story you tell yourself, you experience a feeling—anger, sadness, happiness, relief, surprise, confusion, and so on. *Your feeling is not based on what happened but on your interpretation of what happened.* In terms of what kind of story you tell yourself from the incoming information, your brain's natural inclination is to[19,20]

- Make you look good and feel good about yourself

- Make the other person look like the jerk or the villain

- Cast the people you like most as "good guys" and those you like least as "bad guys"

- Interpret things the way you have in the past—even when you are wrong

- Make it seem as if what's going on in the present is consistent with the past—even in situations where this is not true

- Create a unifying theme so that you can organize and predict events in your life—even when the events are in fact not related and not predictable

- Try to convince yourself that there is a cause-and-effect relationship—even in situations where the events are actually random and unrelated

All these tendencies also apply to the way you create and interpret your memories. The information you choose to store and to remember and the information you choose not to store and not to remember are affected by your initial beliefs, expectations, interpretations, and self-created stories. This means that your memories and the meaning you give to those memories are not always as reliable, as objective, or as accurate as you might think. So as you think about the impact your memories have on your present relationship with your father, consider these surprising research facts:[17-22]

- We can "remember" things that never actually happened because we have been influenced by what other people have told us about the past.

- We sometimes remember things very differently from the way they actually happened.

- Many memories are influenced by what other people have told us about the past—not by what we actually saw or heard ourselves.

- We tend to forget the bad things and remember good things about people we love most.

- We tend to forget good things and remember bad things about people we dislike or are angry with.

- The way we remember another person or an event is affected by our present motives, present goals, and present feelings.

- We are more likely to distort our memories and to twist the facts when our family is dealing with serious, ongoing problems (alcoholism, adultery, divorce, physical abuse, incest, mental illness, or a miserable marriage).

- The way someone words a question affects what we can and cannot remember.

Three Daughters: Why We Believe What Isn't So

All this research about memory and perception means simply this: We often believe what isn't so about our fathers. In the case of Rebecca, Rachel, and Robin, the same "facts" about each of their fathers lead each daughter to an entirely different "truth."

As Rebecca was growing up, her family believed that dad should earn all the money while mom raised the kids. Her family also believed that mothers were more skilled than fathers when it came to raising daughters and that females were "naturally" supposed to be more talkative and involved with each other. Rebecca explained that her dad had always spent 60 to 70 hours a week working, never took a vacation without bringing work along, and seldom asked her what was going on in her life (the data her brain allowed to enter). To her this proved that he had never been as interested in her as her mother was and that he couldn't possibly relate as well to her as her mother did (unflattering interpretation of the data). When I asked if she could remember times when he did try to talk about personal things or show an interest in her, she frowned and said, "Well, yes, but I'm sure he only did that because my mom made him" (tells herself a negative story about a positive fact). Rebecca's perceptions of the "facts" have left her feeling resentful and distant from her father (a negative emotional reaction to the story she tells herself).

Now consider Rachel, whose family's beliefs and father's situation were almost identical to Rebecca's. The difference is that Rachel interprets the "facts" about her dad in a more flattering way. Her interpretation of the facts goes like this: "Yeah, my dad worked almost all the time, even on vacations. That's always made me sad. Actually I feel sorry for dad because even when he tried to spend time with me, he was usually exhausted or preoccupied with work. I knew he loved me, and I wish he'd spent more time with me. But partly I blame my mom. With her education, she could have gotten a good job and taken some of the pressure off dad so that he and I could have had more time together." Again, the basic facts in each daughter's situation are the same, but the way they interpreted those facts left one daughter feeling sad and sorry for her dad and the other feeling resentful.

Then there's Robin. Her family had been dealing with one tough situation after another for years. She remembers her father drinking heavily, even though he was a successful lawyer. Just before she graduated from high school, her dad left her mother. Afterwards, her mother became clinically depressed and then intensely angry after Robin's dad remarried. Her brother also struggled with depression during this time. Robin's memories and interpretations went something like this: "The divorce was 100 percent his fault, and so is my mother's and brother's depression. My mom never did a single thing wrong in that marriage to deserve this. Besides, I can't remember dad doing anything loving for me while I was growing up except taking me to Disneyland once. And he never once contacted me after he remarried." Initially not a single memory of her father was positive, whereas her memories of her mom were overwhelmingly positive. I also noticed the extreme words she used to describe events: *never, always, 100 percent, completely.* In her memory, her dad was the powerful villain—and everyone else was a powerless victim.

As I talked to Robin over the next few months, I worded my questions in ways that might help her to recall something good about her dad. Sure enough, the good began to surface. She did remember that her mom had been diagnosed as clinically depressed long before her parents divorced. She also recalled that her brother had been a difficult, emotionally troubled child all during her parents' marriage. As you might expect, she also remembered that her father had done many loving things other than taking her to Disneyland. But the memory that unnerved her the most was this: Her father had phoned and written to her and her brother for the first year or two after he remarried. But both kids had refused to have anything to do with him given the suffering that they felt he had caused everyone. Fortunately, Robin was shaken up enough by these memories that she decided to contact her father after not having spoken to him for several years. The outcome shocked her because her father's response contradicted most of her memories and her beliefs about him. As she wrote in her most recent e-mail to me: "He said my contacting him was the best gift I had ever given him. I always had this vision of him as some opinionated, overbearing, stubborn tyrant. It has always been unthinkable to me that he might admit his failures. But he has. And I know he does love me and always did."

In telling you these three stories, I am not saying that you can't rely on anything you remember. And I'm not saying that your father was always the hero and never the villain. If you remember him being a jerk at times, I'm sure you're right—at least partially right and at least some of the time. What I'm trying to get you focused on is this: Your memories and your interpretations of what happened in the past are not 100 percent accurate or 100 percent reliable.

Now What?

Now that we've seen how our beliefs, perceptions, and memories can mislead us, what advice am I giving you? How can you use this research to strengthen your relationship with your father?

First, keep reminding yourself that your memories and interpretations of the past are not necessarily accurate, complete, or unbiased. Your father's interpretations and his memories are just as valid as yours because both of you have filtered the information and given it meaning based on your own beliefs, biases, and expectations. There is his reality and your reality—his truth and your truth—his interpretations and your interpretations—his facts and your facts. Ultimately, there is no way to judge which of you is right. There is no winner or no loser because there is no way to figure out which person collected and processed the information the most accurately. What is important for the sake of your relationship is that you realize that both you and your father do make mistakes in the ways you remember and interpret the past.

If some of your memories are still hurting your relationship with your father in some way, it's worth exploring just how accurate those memories are. Ask yourself: Who could I get more information from about that particular situation? What information might be missing from my version of the story? Is there a more positive way I could interpret that situation now that I'm older? Is there anyone who might have encouraged me to remember that incident in such a negative way? If so, what might have motivated that person to want me to see my dad in a bad light?

Consider what Jessica did with my advice. For years she had felt that her dad favored her brother and enjoyed being with him more than with her. (Remember, a feeling is based on the kind of story you tell yourself about those particular "facts" your filter allowed to enter your brain.) Two things stood out most in her memory: Her dad rarely showed up for her gymnastics tournaments, and he never took her camping like he did with her brother, even though she begged him to repeatedly. To start, she needed to be sure that she had her facts right, so she asked her brother and each of her parents how often they remembered her dad coming to her gymnastics and taking her camping. She did this when she had each of them alone so that their responses weren't affected by what anyone else might remember. Sure enough, all three of them confirmed her facts. But her mom also casually remarked, "When your dad used to say he wanted to take you camping, I told him I didn't think it looked right for you two to go off alone like that because people might get the wrong impression since you were a teenage girl." That one new piece of information put a whole new spin on things for Jennifer. Next, without being threatening or judgmental, she asked her dad questions about those camping trips and the gymnastics. As he talked, the story and memories she had been clinging to for years began to change. He said, "It really made me sad that I had to miss so many of your gymnastics events because they scheduled most of them on the nights that I was required to work late. You were always so much easier to be around than your brother. Maybe that's why it really drained me spending so much time with him when he was a teenager. I kept hoping I could help him become a happier person like you were."

Aha! Bingo! Jessica's memory had been correct *but not complete*. And her interpretation of the facts had been all wrong. Her dad's remarks triggered some other memories that she hadn't mixed into the overall picture. True, her brother had been a very difficult person to be around as a teenager. But she had assumed (wrongly) that he must have been transformed into "superson" when he went off with her dad because the two of them kept going on those camping trips. True, her dad had always looked drained when he got home from those camping weekends. But she interpreted this to mean that he was tired from all the fun he'd had with "superson." In the end, Jessica took the same facts and memories that she had started with and gave them a new interpretation—one that drew her and her father closer.

Facing Facts about Fathers

Many of the beliefs and expectations we have about our fathers as we're growing up are based on what we see or hear in the media instead of being based on nationwide statistics or research drawn from large numbers of people. Two of these beliefs are fairly widespread—and especially damaging to father-daughter relationships. The first is that a daughter's relationship with her father doesn't need to be as communicative, as involved, or as emotionally intimate as her relationship with her mother. The second is that most fathers are not as insightful, as wise, or as skilled as mothers when it comes to raising daughters. Sadly, these two beliefs are reflected in many TV shows and commercials,[23,24] greeting cards and movies,[23] and children's books.[25,26] Even professionals with the most education and the most experience working with or studying families (school counselors, family therapists, researchers, and textbook authors) too often pay less attention to fathers and to father-daughter relationships than to mothers or mother-daughter relationships.[27,28]

Again, remember: *Our beliefs influence the way we treat our fathers and the way they treat us even when those beliefs are not based on facts.* Despite the messages conveyed by so much of our media, our best research and recent statistics show that fathers and daughters benefit by having just as close, as open, and as emotionally intimate a relationship as mothers and daughters. And fathers have many unique skills and special insights as parents—especially with daughters. In fact, a father usually has *more* impact than a mother on certain aspects of their daughter's life—her work, her relationships with men, and her self-reliance. And even after the father dies, his influence over his daughter's life continues—sometimes more powerfully than when he was alive. As a gypsy proverb puts it, "You can never dig deep enough to 'bury' your father."

Your challenge is to ditch the beliefs you grew up with that have limited your relationship with your father—beliefs that have blinded you to the facts and realities about most fathers. Start by considering the following aspects of your life where your father generally has as much or more impact than your mother:[27-30]

- Achieving academic and career success—especially in math and science

- Maintaining a loving, trusting, communicative relationship with a man

- Dealing well with people in authority—especially men

- Being socially, sexually, and intellectually confident

- Developing self-reliance and initiative

- Being willing to try new things and to accept challenges

- Maintaining good mental health (no clinical depression, eating disorders, or chronic anxiety)

- Being able to empathize with others

- Recognizing and accepting your own imperfections

- Expressing anger comfortably and appropriately—especially with men

I know that it's hard to accept facts or research that challenges certain beliefs with which you've grown up. This is why in every chapter I'm giving you "Eye Openers" to help you to expand your vision of fathers. If you feel yourself getting upset as you're reading the "Eye Openers," try calming down by asking yourself: Why are these facts upsetting me so much? Am I reacting this way because I'm feeling guilty for mistreating or misjudging my father in some way? What might it mean for my relationship with him if I allow myself to accept this new information?

Removing Your Blindfolds

I'm hoping you've decided that you want to reexamine some of the beliefs and perceptions that may be limiting your relationship with your dad. You can start by teaching yourself to recognize the negative messages about fathers that surround you. When you learn to do this, it's like putting on a powerful pair of glasses. With your improved vision, your relationship with your dad is less likely to be limited by negative assumptions or false beliefs about fathers. When you learn to recognize the negative messages, you can stand back and ask yourself: Wait a minute, how accurate is that negative message? How true is that insulting assumption? How many fathers are that stupid, that insensitive, or that selfish in real life? What's the other side to this story? How would I feel if that message was about mothers instead of fathers?

Here's one way to sharpen your vision: Think about your favorite television programs, commercials, children's books, magazines, and movies. Now ask yourself: What kind of relationship does the daughter usually have with her father compared with her mother? Which parent is usually the most involved, most attentive, most understanding, most approachable, and most nurturing? If either parent does something that hurts the family, which parent is the worst? How often are the father and daughter doing something alone? Which parent usually knows the most about what's going on in the children's lives—especially the daughter's? Which parent is usually teaching the spouse how to do things the "right way" with the kids? If there is no father present, why isn't there? Is the father usually taking care of the family or expressing love by buying things for them—life insurance, cars, a bigger house, a vacation—instead of just nurturing them emotionally?

Remove your blindfolds by exposing yourself to more positive images of fathers. You can do this by reading books (especially children's books), watching movies, and visiting Web sites that offer loving, nurturing images of fathers. Many of my favorites are in the following box.

Expanding Your Vision of Fathers

Photographic Essays

Fathers and Daughters in Their Own Words[31]

Father Songs[32]

Fatherhood in Black America[33]

Fathers: A Celebration[34]

Children's Books

Daddy Will Be There[35]

I Live with Daddy[36]

Night Shift Daddy[37]

Movies

To Kill a Mockingbird

Father of the Bride

Parenthood

Eat Drink, Man, Woman

A Soldier's Daughter Never Cries

Guess Who's Coming to Dinner

One True Thing

Ordinary People

The Young Girl and the Monsoon

Web Sites

Center of Successful Fathering: *fathering.org*

Dads and Daughters: *dadsanddaughters.org*

Father and Child Society: *fatherandchild.org*

Fathers Direct: *fathersdirect.com*

Fathering Magazine: *fathermag.com*

Fathers Resource Center: *fathersresourcecenter.org*

Father's Web: *fathering.com*

Men's Stuff Center: *menstuff.org*

National Center for Fathering: *fathers.com*

The Fatherhood Project: *fatherhoodproject.org*

The Men's Center: *themenscenter.com*

In closing, I want to urge you to think carefully about the "Eye Openers" in the following chapters. Allow these eye-opening facts to expand your vision of fathers—especially your own. And always keep in mind: What you have been taught to believe about fathers and about father-daughter relationships influences the way you treat your father—even when your beliefs are not based on reality or facts.

Chapter 2

Dad: More Than a Wallet
Learning to Bank on Yourself

- Have you and your father ever had disagreements or tensions related to money?

- Have you felt that you've disappointed him in regard to your education or your work?

- Do you think that he let you or your family down in any way when it came to work or money?

- Did you ever feel that he was uptight or too worried about work or money?

- Do you feel that he interfered with or was too critical of your plans or your decisions?

If you answered yes to any of these questions, then money and work have had an impact on your relationship—and probably not a good one. I'm not just talking here about your dad's work or his money but also about your work and your money. Money creates tension for many of us in our closest relationships.[1] This is so because money stirs up all kinds of feelings—jealousy, resentment, rivalry, insecurity, shame, guilt, appreciation, love, joy, and obligation. In most relationships, money also represents power—who has the most of it, what they do with it, and how others react to it. As the old sayings go, "When we claim that it's *not* the money that matters but rather the *principle* of the thing, it usually *is* the money!" So let's see how money and work have played a part in your father-daughter relationship.

Your Family's Beliefs

I know we've been over this already, but it's worth repeating: What you and your father have been taught to believe about fathers and daughters has a big impact on how you treat each other and what you expect from each other—even when the beliefs you started with are not true. And many of the beliefs that affect your father-daughter relationship are related to work and money. Use the following quiz to focus on what your family believed while you were growing up.

Fooling Yourself? Men, Work, Family

During most of the years you were growing up, what did your parents believe—and which of their beliefs did you share? In addressing the following statements, use 0 for "false" and 1 for "true."

Me Dad Mom

___ ___ ___ Most men enjoy being at work as much as being with their kids.

___ ___ ___ When both parents work full time, fathers spend much less time with kids than mothers.

___ ___ ___ In the United States men traditionally have earned all the family's income while women raised the kids.

___ ___ ___ Most men are just as free as women to choose the kind of work they want to do.

___ ___ ___ Most parents and children are happier when the husband earns all of the income.

___ ___ ___ Most fathers enjoy their jobs more than most employed mothers do.

___ ___ ___ Kids are usually better adjusted when their mother is a full-time homemaker.

___ ___ ___ A mother is usually happier and more fulfilled when her husband earns all of the family's money.

___ ___ ___ Employed mothers are more stressed than fathers trying to balance work and family.

___ ___ ___ Fathers and daughters usually have closer relationships when the mother is a full-time homemaker.

___ ___ ___ Score (10 possible)

If your family's scores were higher than 7, your beliefs about men, work, and money have detracted in certain ways from your father-daughter relationship. You'll see what I mean as you read this chapter. For now, just focus on this: None of the statements in the quiz are true. That's right—not a single one. So the higher your family's scores, the more you'll want to think about this: How did believing these untrue things affect my relationship with my dad? If my family had not believed these things, how might my relationship with my father have been different— then and now? As you think about your family's beliefs, consider these eye-opening realities:

Eye Openers

- Fathers are just as stressed as mothers are in trying to balance work and family.[2,3]
- Historically in our country, *both* parents have worked to support the family, and 80 percent of all parents still do.[4]
- Fathers are often closer to their kids later in life when men are under less pressure to earn money.[5,6]
- Many fathers wish their jobs allowed them to spend more time with their kids.[3,7]
- The more hours a mother works and the higher her income, the more time the father spends with their kids and on household chores.[9-11]
- Employed mothers are usually happier and more fulfilled than full-time housewives.[12,13]
- Father and daughter usually have a closer relationship when the mother has a full-time job while the children are growing up.[12-15]

Your Parents' Decisions

Whatever beliefs your parents had about work and money led them to make decisions that have affected the kind of relationship you and your father now have. Consider these two daughters and their fathers.

Meredith

Long before her parents ever met, Meredith's future mother had made the decision not to pursue a career that would be too exhausting or demanding. Instead, she chose to work at jobs that were very satisfying personally, although the pay wasn't very high. After she married, she worked full time while her young husband finished his last year in law school. As expected of him since he was a boy, he carried on his family's tradition and fulfilled his own father's dream—every son a lawyer or doctor. When Meredith was born, her mom quit work while her dad climbed his way up to become a partner in a top-notch law firm. This meant that he had to work 60 to 70 hours a week and commute almost 2 hours a day to the city so that his family could live "the good life" in the suburbs. Most weekends he had to bring work home. And on vacations he usually had to take his laptop computer, answer e-mails, and occasionally cut the vacation short for a crisis back at work. The commuting became so exhausting that he eventually had to rent an apartment in the city. So from the time that Meredith was 10, her father was home only on weekends. At the early age of 57, Meredith's father was able to retire, having given all three kids expensive college educations, cars, and extravagant weddings. This is how Meredith describes their relationship: "I know dad loves me but I can't imagine our talking about anything personal. To be honest, he doesn't know much at all about what's going on in my life. I guess he never really did. As a teenager, I felt he was sort of intruding on the family since he only came home from the city on the weekends."

Jeannette

Long before Jeanette was born, her mother had established a reputation as one of the best hair stylists in town. She married a high school teacher, and they had four children. Jeannette's mom continued working full time, including most Saturdays and two evenings until 6 o'clock. Of course, this meant that dad spent the most time with the kids because he had summers and Saturdays off and got home each afternoon around 4 o'clock. When Jeannette went to college, she had to take out loans to pay her way. She and her fiancée also had to pay for their own wedding because none of the parents could afford to help out. Needless to say, at the age of 57, Jeannette's dad was nowhere near being able to think about retiring. And this is how Jeannette describes their relationship: "I'm actually closer to my dad than to my mom. I guess it's because we spent more time together while I was growing up, especially when I got home from school in the afternoons. I'd say he's one of my best friends."

The point of these two stories isn't that one father made the right choice while the other blundered. In fact, you and some other daughter may not necessarily agree on which father actually made the better choice. The point is that the type of work a man chooses to do—or feels that he must do in order to make other people happy—has a major impact on the kind of relationship he and his children develop over the years. This isn't to say that all parents who work long hours or who have stressful, demanding jobs fail to develop close relationships with their children—or that all parents whose jobs allow them to spend plenty of time with their kids turn out with great relationships. But the fact remains: It is more difficult for you and your parent to develop a close relationship or to get to know each other well when that parent works long hours or is the major wage earner for your family—and in most families, that parent is the father.

If your parents are like most adults in our country, they were raised to believe that it's a father's responsibility to make most—or all—of the family's money. Your dad felt that it was "natural" to prepare himself for the highest-paying jobs—and "natural" that he would not get to spend as much time with his kids as his wife would. Do you wonder if your father ever felt: "This isn't fair. I'd have liked to have been free to choose a less stressful job instead of the one that paid the most. I'd have liked to have been able to take a part-time job or to quit work for a few years and stay home with my kids. I'd have liked to have been able to take a job that was more fulfilling, even though it paid less." In any case, as you can see from the "Eye Openers" below, most fathers have less time to spend with their children than most mothers because of the kind of work most men do.

My point isn't to criticize your parents—or anyone else's parents—for the kinds of choices they make about work or money. When they were young, I doubt that either of your parents thought much about how their

Eye Openers[3,8]

- Two million fathers stay home to raise their children while their wives work.
- Eighty percent of the fathers in our country earn most of the money for their families.
- Counting the time spent commuting, working, doing house and yard work, and being with the kids, the average father has 5 hours *less* free time each week than the average mother.
- Almost 60 percent of mothers with children under the age of one and almost 75 percent with children older than one are employed.
- Fathers' jobs generally involve more physical risk, more stress, and more traveling and commuting than mothers' jobs.
- On average, employed fathers work 10 more hours a week than employed mothers.

decisions would affect your father-daughter relationship years later. Before your father and your mother got together, I doubt that your father was saying to himself: "Let's see now. If I want to have lots of time with my future daughter, I better marry a woman who will work just as many hours and earn just as much money as I do." And I doubt that your mother was thinking: "I better not marry a man who has to be away from our daughter much more than I do earning money for our family." My point is simply this: The kinds of decisions your parents made about work and money are closely tied to the kind of relationship you and your dad have—and the decisions you make will shape the kind of relationship your daughter will have with her father. So how have your parents' decisions affected your relationship with your dad?

Men's Money, Women's Love

If only one thought sticks with you after reading this chapter, I want it to be this: *Many men believe that women's feelings for them are partly—or sometimes largely—based on money.* If your father is like most other men, he is *afraid—*

afraid that women won't like him as much, might leave him more quickly, or might criticize or withdraw from him emotionally if he doesn't earn "enough" money. This is true whether we're talking about working-class men or college-educated men, white or nonwhite, young or old, West Coast or East Coast, or big city or small town. Because this reality may make us women a little uncomfortable—or maybe even a little defensive— I'm going to repeat it. Men often feel that money is *very* important to the women in their lives—their mothers, girlfriends, wives, ex-wives, and *daughters*. As the saying goes, "When his money stops coming through the door, her love flies out the window." Maybe you're thinking to yourself, "What a terrible thing to say about women." "It's nonsense." "I've never been like that." "My feelings for my dad have absolutely nothing to do with his money." You may be right—or you may be fooling yourself. It doesn't really matter. What *you* believe and what *you* feel isn't the point. What matters is: *This is what many men feel and what they fear. This is their reality and their experience.*[16-19]

Men's feelings and fears about women and money have a lot to do with what goes on in your father-daughter relationship. As author and researcher Warren Farrell explains, fathers could be more involved with their wives and daughters if we convinced men and women that men should be loved and desired for who they *are*, not for what they *do*. Farrell recommends raising our daughters to be financially self-reliant and to use some of their own money for dating instead of raising them to expect, want, or rely on men's money. He also suggests that if we're going to tell girls to beware of boys because all they're after is sex, we ought to warn boys to beware of girls because all they're after is the things his money can buy.[19]

Many daughters tell me that they have no idea where their father would get the idea that his income could have any impact on how his daughter or his wife feels about him. To help you to see things from a man's perspective, I'd like you to do these two things: Watch the commercials and programs on prime-time TV, and think about the movies you have seen in recent years. Consider the following because they were so popular with millions of Americans: *My Big Fat Greek Wedding* (the number 1 money-making romantic comedy of all time), *Pretty Woman* (number 2 money-making romantic comedy), *Maid in Manhattan, An Officer and a Gentlemen, First Wives Club, Father of the Bride, Betsy's Wedding,* and *The Sopranos.* Now ask yourself: How much pleasure do the daughters, girlfriends, or wives seem to be getting from the expensive things the man is buying—an expensive wedding, engagement ring, designer clothes, fancy restaurants, nice vacations, a big house, or the freedom to quit her boring job? Is there anything that might give men the impression that women, including their own daughters, might find them more fun to be with, or compliment them more, or pay more attention to them if they have plenty of money? Since we'd think she was crude, bratty, or materialistic if she actively pursued a man or badgered her father for his money, the women in these films "accidentally" meet these men—or the father "voluntarily" gives his daughter a $50,000 wedding. As one writer cleverly puts it, "She is never saving diligently to pay for the $600 ticket to the charity event that will afford her access to the sort of men who might spirit her away from her tiny apartment with a bathtub three inches away from the toaster oven."[20] In any case, you may be asking yourself: What does any of this have to do with me and my dad? Well, let's see.

The Impact of Your Father's Job

Let's start by stepping back into your childhood. As you take the quiz on page 27, think back to what your father has done for a living since you were born. Don't focus only on your father's most recent or his present job.

If your score is higher than 30, your father's work and issues related to money have detracted from your relationship. If your score is less than 10, your father's job and financial issues probably haven't affected your relationship in a negative way. We are going to wait until Chapter 5 to discuss your feelings about the way your dad treated your mother, so let's look now at some of your other concerns.

Workaholic Dad

I can't tell you how many times I've heard daughters say that their dads spent too much time working and not enough time with the family—regardless of whether their dads were college-educated men or blue-collar workers. I rarely meet a daughter who can't remember times when her dad wasn't at

My Father's Job—Burden or Blessing?

In addressing the following statements, use 0 to mean "never," 1 to mean "rarely," 2 to mean "fairly often," and 3 to mean "almost always."

In my opinion, my father

____ focused too much on his job and too little on our family.

____ was too focused on making money.

____ seemed exhausted, preoccupied, or grumpy when he got home.

____ complained about our not appreciating him enough for what he gave us.

____ complained or scolded us for spending too much money.

____ spent less time with me than my mother did.

____ was uptight or tense about money or work.

____ seemed dissatisfied or unhappy with his job.

____ let out family down financially.

____ didn't care as much as he should have about money.

____ seemed to enjoy his work as much or more than being with us.

____ was rude or insensitive to my mother when he came home from work.

____ Total score (36 possible)

some special event or wasn't there for her when she needed him because he was at work. Many say that their fathers are workaholics—an unflattering word implying that he is addicted to a bad thing. What's damaging, though, is your blaming or resenting your father instead of appreciating or feeling sorry for him. Sadly, most daughters feel that their workaholic dad has let them down: "Dad wasn't around enough while I was growing up." "Mom raised us, not him." "He seemed more interested in his job than in us." "He should have spent more time with me instead of buying things for me." "Making money is what mattered most to him." "He didn't *have to* work that hard." "Nobody *forced him* to take such a demanding job." "He could have *chosen to* make less money and spend more time with me." Even if you never felt this way, I'll bet you know other daughters who have.

Materialistic Dad

You also might be a daughter who blames her father for being too materialistic. You think he cares too much about making money, buying lots of "stuff," or being a big show-off. You assume he values material things as much as (or more than) he values you and your family. You may even think less of him because you don't like the way he spends his money. You'd rather he spend it on things that didn't make his wealth quite so obvious to everyone. As some daughters put it, "He's selfish and childish for spending all that money on a luxury sports car." "I hate the way he's Mr. Show-Off with the big house, all the wines, the fancy kitchen." "He embarrasses me because he's always pointing out how much he's spent on things."

In order to feel better about your dad, try to figure out why money and material things seem to mean so much to him. Ask yourself: Could my father possibly have gotten the impression that anyone in our family values him more because he can buy all these fine things for us? Have his parents, his siblings, or any woman he dated before he got married acted as if they were proud of him or admired him *because* he was so successful financially. Does anyone in our family ever become overjoyed or ever say "I love you—you're so wonderful!" to my dad when he gives them pricey things—a vacation, a big wedding, a car, summer study abroad, a computer, plane tickets to come for a visit, a wide-screen TV, or jewelry? When dad has screwed up in some way, does anyone in our family forgive him more quickly if he gives them a gift or expect him to apologize by buying something for them? Am I seeing him as materialistic just because his "stuff" is more visible or more obviously expensive (a supersized refrigerator, a wine cellar, expensive art, or a horse) than my "stuff" (overseas travel, ski equipment, top-of-the-line hiking boots, makeup, hair stylist, or clothes)? Is dad really that much more interested in material things than everyone else in our family?

Lazy or Foolish Dad

The flip side of these complaints is being disappointed or resenting your dad for not working hard enough or for making so many bad financial decisions. In your eyes he has let the family down by lacking ambition, wasting his talents, or not planning well enough for your family's financial future—including your college education. Maybe you blame him because your mom had to get job, or because she was always so stressed out about money, or because they don't have enough to retire. Maybe you resent him for chasing after all those "get rich quick" schemes that never went anywhere or for gambling on so many risky business ventures. Or maybe you see him as an immature dreamer who never grew up—building castles in the air without building foundations under them on the ground. Did you see him as bitter, resentful, or self-pitying instead of as someone who tried even harder when he lost a job or got passed over for promotion? It's possible that you're still upset or embarrassed by him because your family had so much less than most of the people you knew or had to borrow money from relatives. As you grow older, do you resent him because you may end up having to give him or your mother money because he didn't plan ahead well enough? If you've ever felt this way about your father, you may feel less resentful after asking yourself: Would I feel this disappointed in him if he had been the female parent instead of the male parent? In what ways is our relationship better than it might be if he had been a huge financial success? What about my father's upbringing might have made it so difficult for him to become successful?

Overshadowed, Hidden Dad

Too many daughters draw the wrong conclusions about their fathers because they've made two very understandable mistakes. First, they base too many of their opinions of dad on the way he behaves when he is preoccupied with or exhausted from work. Second, they assume that the way dad behaves at work is the way he is going to behave toward them.

As young kids, very few of us understand that the way dad behaves when he gets home from work is not the best way to judge how he feels about us—or the best way to assess his personality. As we are growing up, we too often judge dad when he is at his *worst*—at the end of his work day when he is most exhausted, frustrated, preoccupied, uptight, or spaced out. Without a chance to unwind, presto! He's supposed to transform himself into the opposite of what he's had to be at work all day—intense, focused, serious, logical, precise, or responsible for solving everyone's problems. Or he's worn out from the physical labor, the people grumbling at him for things that weren't his fault, or the boss treating him like a bumbling idiot. But as a child you wanted the magic to begin as soon as dad came through the door: It's a bird. It's a plane. No, it's Super Dad—a light-hearted, playful, laid-back, affectionate, energetic, talkative, attentive parent who gives you and the rest of the family the attention you need.

Now that you're older, you probably have a much better understanding of what your dad felt like when he got home from work. I doubt that you want anyone judging your personality or assessing how you feel about them on the basis of the way you behave at the end of an exhausting day at work. Let's face it, many of us just want to unwind without having anyone else make any demands on us when we first get home from work. If you're still in school, consider the way you treat the people you love most when you're in the middle of exam week or when you just find out that you failed a big test. Now that we're older, we daughters need to ask ourselves: Which of my negative impressions of my father have been based mainly on how he behaved when he was preoccupied or exhausted from work? How can I get to know my father better and see the other aspects of him that have been overshadowed by his job? (In Chapter 4 we're going to answer this.)

Let's take a closer look at your dad at the end of his workday. Thinking back to your childhood, imagine your dad after he gets home from work. How did he look most of the time when he came in the door? What was the expression on his face? What was his tone of voice? What did he do first? What did he say? How did he treat you, your mom, or your family pet? What are you feeling about him? What kind of person did he seem to be? Let these words prod your memory: relaxed, playful, silly, cheerful, peppy, loving, calm, attentive, appreciative, affectionate, laid back, sweet, upbeat, conversational, and focused on the family or uptight, tense, grumpy, pooped, inattentive, distant, cold, picky, preoccupied, disinterested, bossy, defensive, touchy, demanding, critical, high strung, withdrawn, argumentative, confrontational, and off in space somewhere. Was he easily upset by the loud TV, the dog peeing on the floor, the bike left in the middle of the driveway, the messy house, dinner not being ready, the chores you forgot to do, or the missing parts of the newspaper? Overall, what kind of person did you think he was based on how he acted when he got home?

The second mistake we make is assuming that the way our father behaves at work is the way he's going to behave toward us. For example, if his job requires him to act extremely confident, competitive, outspoken, and decisive, you might assume that he isn't capable of being vulnerable, emotional, confused, or humble around you. Or the kind of work he did while you were growing up may have led you to believe that he couldn't be very insightful, communicative, sensitive, or tender with you.

Are you getting the feeling that maybe you have misjudged your dad at times by jumping to negative conclusions about him based on the kind of work he does or his behavior when he's preoccupied or exhausted from work? If so, the next two chapters will offer you plenty of ideas for getting to know your father more fully.

Exploring Your Father's Experiences

If your father's job has detracted from or interfered with your relationship at any point, what can you do about it now? First, I'd suggest that you invite your father to watch films with you about men's struggles to balance work and family, to cope with the stress of being the main wage earner, and to deal with failure at work. As you watch these films together, ask your father if he ever felt like the men in these movies—or if he ever knew other men who had experiences similar to those in the films. If you can't actually watch the films together, each of you can watch them on your own and then talk about them by phone afterwards. Here are some of the films I recommend as good conversation starters about fathers and work: *Nobody's Fool, Glengarry Glen Ross, Death of a Salesman, The Big Kahuna, The Big Night, Spring Forward,* and *One True Thing.* You also can talk to your father about the "Eye Openers" and quizzes in this chapter.

Now go on a fact-finding mission by getting your dad to talk about his experiences and his feelings about work and family. Ask him to talk about the work he has done since you were born, the times he might have felt stressed by having to make money for your family, and the times he resented having to work because he couldn't be with you. I don't think you'll get very far asking broad, general questions such as, "Dad, tell me about your work. Do you ever feel like the family banking machine?" Most daughters get to know their fathers much better by asking questions such as the ones listed in the following box. In the next chapter I'm going to explain how to approach your father and how to ask questions in ways that will draw him out. At this point, just remember: If your father is like many other men, he is *afraid* that money plays a big part in how you feel about him—afraid that you won't be as pleased with him, won't admire him as much, won't pay as much attention to him, or won't want to spend as much time with him if he doesn't earn "enough" money.

It is also time to reexamine some of the stories you've been telling yourself about your father. This means using the information you gather from him

---

Work and Money: Questions for My Father

1. When you were young, what did you hope for in your life in terms of work and money?
2. What people or circumstances influenced the type of work you chose?
3. If the money hadn't mattered at all, what kind of work would you have chosen?
4. What have you liked least and most about your work over the years?
5. What advice would you give me about work, money, and happiness?
6. How well does your job fit your personality?
7. How has your work affected your life at home?
8. How has your work affected your relationship with me?
9. What do you hope for me in terms of work and money?
10. How do your parents or other relatives feel about the work you do?
11. How do you define success, and how successful do you think you are?

12. What are the biggest mistakes you've made related to work or money?
13. How has your work turned out differently from what you wanted as a young man?
14. If you had been a woman, what kind of work would you have chosen and why?
15. If you had to have chosen another type of work, what would it have been?
16. What have you been proudest of in your work?
17. What has disappointed you most since you first went to work as an adult?
18. How much pleasure has your work given you over the years?
19. How would you feel if your wife had always earned much more money than you do?
20. How would you feel about my marrying a man who earns much less than I do?
21. What have you lost or had to give up over the years because of your work?
22. What do you wish you had known about work and money when you were younger?
23. How do you feel about the kind of work your father did, and how did that affect your choices?
24. If you could afford to retire now, would you? What would you do with your time?
25. How have people misunderstood you in terms of your work or money?

to change some of the negative perceptions you may have had of him regarding work and money. After asking their fathers the questions in the preceding box, here is how some daughters' perceptions changed for the better:

- "My dad actually told me that if he could do it all again, he wouldn't work for a big corporation and make all this money. It's funny because for all these years I've thought he loved his work and that it was just normal for dads never to be at home."

- "Until I asked him these questions, I always thought he just didn't care about being away from me so much."

- "For the first time in my life I learned how trapped my dad has always felt as the provider. As successful and well known as he is, I was stunned."

- "As we talked, I understood why he didn't like it that my mom made more money than him. Now I see that he wasn't being jealous or competitive or mean to her. He just felt like a loser."

- "I can't believe I had never thought about what it was like for him to commute 2 hours to work for 23 years to a city and a job he hated."

- "I was in shock when he told me that he had given up a higher-paying job to spend more time with us kids when I was young. I'd always thought of him as being pretty selfish. I wish I'd known this sooner."

- "I was always acutely aware of his obsession with money. I remember him falling apart when checks would bounce or my mother would take us back-to-school shopping. Mom would always get mad and brush him off. So my sisters and I never took him seriously. After listening to him talk about the financial hardships in his childhood, I felt a pang of guilt as I look back on how selfish the four of us girls must have seemed to him."

- "As I let him talk, I realized that at his law firm my dad is expected to have certain qualities because he's in charge of so many people. At work he shows confidence and intelligence by giving direct, strong, immediate answers. The slightest hesitation on his part would diminish his clients' and colleagues' confidence in him. I've always felt he wasn't taking my problems seriously because he's always communicated that same way with me—his lawyer style. But now I have a new appreciation for his honesty and directness. I see that he is listening."

Eye Openers[21-23]

- American parents and their adult children run up far more debt and save less money than people in other industrialized nations.
- The average American works 70 more hours a year than the average Japanese and 350 hours more than the average European.
- Many of us judge what's going on in a relationship by how much money each person is spending on the other.
- Most Americans consider it perfectly normal to live their entire lives in debt.

Now here's your next task: Tell your father what you've been discovering. Talk to him about how some of your former ideas about him are changing. As you move forward in your own work, give your dad the chance to be your ally—continue asking him questions about the decisions he made as a younger man, and continue exploring his values and comparing them to your own. Embrace his experiences—allow them to be woven into the fabric of your own life.

Your Attitudes and Behavior: Work and Money

Now that we've seen how your father's decisions about work and money have affected your relationship, let's take a look at your decisions and attitudes. It's been my experience that if there is tension, it exists for at least one of these reasons: (1) You think your father is disappointed in you—your decisions about school, a job, or the way you handle money; (2) you feel that he's criticizing or interfering too much with your plans and decisions; or (3) you and your father didn't agree on what your financial relationship ought to be after you graduate from high school.

Disappointed Dad

Do you feel that your dad is disappointed in you—that he wishes you would do more with your life? Do you feel that you've failed him somehow—or does he feel that he's failed because you weren't able to measure up to his expectations? If so, I'll bet you feel that he criticizes you and compares you with more successful people your age—maybe even your own brother or sister. And I'll bet you both get tense whenever the topic of your future plans or your present job/school "situation" comes up. Daughters tell me that the most helpful questions I ask them are the following: How satisfied are *you* with the decisions you have made so far? How proud are *you* of your present situation at work or at school or with money?

Some daughters tell me that they're very satisfied and proud of themselves. They feel that the choices they've made—or are about to make—are right for them. Their worry is that their father is disappointed in them—or that he's soon going to be—because he has a successful career and an impressive income. "Dad isn't going to like it when I tell him I've taken this lower-paying job." "He's going to get mad when he finds out I've decided not to go on with my education." "I know he's not proud of the kind of work I'm doing." Sound familiar? Then Melissa's story will interest you. Melissa was afraid to let her father know that she wasn't going on to law school. She was really feeling guilty because—you guessed it—her dad was a lawyer. I asked if she had ever approached her dad with the topic. No, she hadn't. Had she ever talked to him about how he felt spending his life as a lawyer? No, she hadn't. Had he ever told her that he wouldn't be able to stand it if she wasn't a lawyer? No, he hadn't. As I explained to her, she was making a lot of negative assumptions about this man *without having given him a chance* to hear about her decision or to share his feelings with her. She was convinced that she "knew" this man. And why? Because she was making the wrong assumptions about him based on the kind of work he did and his income.

So here's what I suggested: Set plenty of time aside to talk to your father about why you've made this decision (in private, with absolutely nobody else around). Tell him that because you love him and because you respect his success, you're often afraid of disappointing him. Tell him how much you appreciate what he has done for you financially. Also tell him what you've told me—that you don't want him to feel that he's wasted his money on your education now that you're not going to be a lawyer. Then be quiet—just let him tell you how he feels. Give him the chance to embrace your decisions. For Melissa, there was a happy ending. Her dad wasn't mad or disappointed. In fact, he ended up telling her some of the things that he hadn't like about being a lawyer. He explained that his acting excited was because she had seemed so excited and he wanted to be supportive. What mattered most to him was her being happy. Of course, there's no guarantee that your dad will react this way. But that's not what matters. What matters most is giving him a chance to hear about your plans and to tell you how he feels *before* you make such negative assumptions about him. Stop prejudging him.

Unfortunately, most daughters who believe that their fathers are disappointed in them aren't like Melissa. Most of them are not satisfied with the decisions they've made or with their present financial, work, or school situation. They tell me such things as: "My job sucks. I didn't make good decisions." "I don't have a clue what I'm going to do now. I have no idea what to tell my dad when he asks what my plans are." "I didn't listen to his advice, and now I'm stuck with no good choices." If you're like these daughters, most of the tension between you and your dad is not caused by his being disappointed in you—but by *you* being disappointed in you. You're so down on yourself that you tend to feel your father is judging or criticizing you even when he isn't. The judgmental voice you hear above all others is *yours*, not his. I'm not saying that your dad might not be disappointed. I'm saying that *most* of the criticism is coming from your own self. Even if he is critical sometimes, his opinions wouldn't have nearly as much impact on your relationship if *you* weren't disappointed in your self or embarrassed by your present situation (work, school, or money).

Here are three suggestions that have worked for many daughters. First, be honest with your father. Let him know that you're disappointed with yourself in certain ways. If you don't have a clue what to do in terms of work or some financial problem, just tell him. (I'm sure he's already figured this out, so it's not as if it's some big disclosure on your part.) Second, tell him that you interpret what he says as criticism because you're so down on yourself already. Also tell him that when you feel criticized, you have a hard time coming to him for advice. Third, ask him if he will wait for you to come to him for advice before he offers it to you. We're going to focus on how to ask your father for advice or for approval in Chapter 3. So just keep these three ideas in mind for now.

Critical, Interfering Dad

Even if you've never felt that your father was disappointed in you, I'll bet there are times when you feel that he's been too critical or has interfered too much with your plans about work, school, or money. Daughters often tell me: "When I talk about my future plans, he points out all the shortcomings of my ideas. Then he asks all these questions about things I haven't thought about yet." "Whatever my decision is, he usually points out why it's not going to work." "He treats me like a child because he's always giving me advice about a better way to carry out my ideas."

What can you do? First, take a good look at what's going on between you and your father when he's trying to give you advice. Since I deal with this at length in Chapter 3, for now, I'll keep it brief. What's going on is this: You want to win his approval and to prove how self-reliant you are, and he wants to nurture and protect you. Odds are your father is not trying to control you, to judge you, or to make you feel foolish. He is trying to guide, help, love, and nurture you. When he tries to steer you in another direction, to modify your plans in any way, or to point out potential risks or flaws, you interpret what he's doing as an attack—an attack on your intelligence, an attack on your independence, or an attack on your personality. *He is trying to treat you like an adult*—to talk to you candidly, to discuss the strengths and weaknesses of your plans, to freely express ideas that differ from yours, and to think things through as rationally and logically as possible. *But at some level you may still want him to treat you like a child*—to say whatever it takes to make you feel good about your ideas, to pretend that your plans are too perfect to be improved on, and to act as if you're his equal when it comes to experience at making decisions about work or money. If that's how your father interacts with you, I'm sure you end up feeling good afterwards. But the reality is that he's treating you like a little girl, not like a woman.

If you want to be treated like a woman, you can't act like a little girl. If you want your father to listen to your ideas and your opinions without interrupting, mocking, or getting angry, then you have to do the same—even though his ideas and opinions aren't the same as yours. If you want him to accept the plans or decisions you're making for yourself, then you need to accept him as someone who isn't your clone—someone with ideas and opinions that differ from yours. When you say that you want him to *accept* or *respect* your plans or decisions, most of the time what you really want is for him to *agree* and to *approve of* them—and that is thinking like a little girl, not like a woman. Enough of this for now. There's more to come in Chapter 3.

Second, put yourself in his place—the no-win situation of a gift giver whose presents are tossed back in his face. If he keeps his mouth shut or nods approvingly at all your ideas and plans, you're bound to make certain mistakes that will cause you pain or trouble. Because he loves you, he wants to prevent that from happening. But if he speaks up, you're likely to get mad or lash out at him: "You're such a control freak—always interfering and criticizing." "Stop treating me like a child!" Either way, he gets hurt—and blamed. Likewise, if he encourages you to do your best, to get more education, or to pursue the highest paying jobs or most prestigious careers, you can blame him at some point if you're not happy: "You shouldn't have pushed me so hard!" "You made me focus on making money instead of on choosing a fulfilling job." Yet you still may end up blaming him if he does the opposite—encouraging you to go into a less demanding line of work, to do whatever brings you pleasure no matter how little it pays, to start a family and work part time, or to give up working altogether and rely on your husband's money. If you're not satisfied, years later you may still lash out at him: "You didn't take my work seriously enough." "You didn't push me hard enough, the way you did my brother." "You should have been more concerned about my education." Sadder and more painful still, he may feel that you're rejecting some of the most precious gifts he wanted to give you—the gift of his experiences, the gift of all he has learned in the world of work. There he is—a man with gifts in hand—for you. But instead of joyfully accepting his gifts and embracing him, you toss them aside—unopened, unwanted, and unappreciated.

Third, instead of seeing your father as judgmental or controlling, think of him as *afraid.* When you feel that he's interfering or is asking you too many questions about your future plans, see a frightened man, not a stern-faced judge. Afraid of what? Afraid that you'll blame him somehow if your choices don't work out well. Afraid that the choices you are making eventually will

Eye Openers[23-26]

Many young adults, even those with college degrees,

- Are depressed or deeply disappointed because their jobs aren't as fulfilling or as much "fun" as they had expected them to be.
- Have very unrealistic ideas about earning, budgeting, and saving money.
- Expect to be richer than dad without having to work harder than he did. [27]
- Have gotten used to a lifestyle on their father's money that they can't afford on their own incomes.
- Live with their parents (as many as 4 million 25- to 34-year-olds), often paying nothing for food or rent. [28]

In addition, families with a total income of more than $62,000 spend roughly $250,000 to raise each child, *not including* college costs. [29]

make *you* unhappy or create financial problems or greater stress for you. He also may be afraid that your decisions some day may have a negative impact on him. If your plans don't work out, will you expect him to help you out financially? If he doesn't volunteer to give you money, will you punish him in some way—withdraw from him emotionally, pout, spend less time with him, or get your mom to talk him into helping you out even if this puts a strain on their relationship? Remember: Many men believe that women love them less if they don't provide money. If your father has any reason at all to believe that you might ever expect him to give you money if your ideas don't work out as planned, read on.

Banking on Dad

How much do you bank on your dad—and I mean literally. How much do you still count on him to help you out or to bale you out financially? I've found that most financial tensions occur because fathers and daughters don't see eye to eye on their financial relationship—what each expects and what each feels is fair. Many haven't even talked about what the cut off is for being an "adult"—being 100 percent on your own financially. The following quiz can help you and your father to identify your expectations—and talk about them. Even if money isn't an issue between you at this point, talking with each other about your answers can help you to see where some of your problems in the past came from—or where potential problems may arise in the future. If this makes you nervous, do it anyway!

Banking on Dad?

How do you and your father feel about these matters? In addressing the following statements, use 0 to mean "absolutely not," 1 to mean "maybe," 2 to mean "probably," and 3 to mean "definitely."

After I graduate from high school, my father should

You Dad

___ ___ continue to pay all my educational and living expenses.

___ ___ loan me money instead of telling me to get a bank loan.

___ ___ pay for my graduate school education or part of it.

___ ___ pay for most (or all) of my wedding.

___ ___ set aside some money for me as an inheritance.

___ ___ let me live at home for free after I've finished school and have a job.

___ ___ help me to make a down payment on a house.

___ ___ pay for most (or all) of my first car.

___ ___ pay for my health and car insurance until I finish my education.

___ ___ offer to give me money when he sees that I'm financially stressed.

___ ___ Your scores (30 possible)

Most of us don't like talking about money with the people we love—whether we're talking about inheritance, the costs of a wedding, or the cost of a college education. In fact, though, the more nervous this idea makes you, the more you need to talk. Not talking about money is usually a recipe for trouble, as many therapists and lawyers warn us. [1, 30]

There are four different combinations of scores that signal problems in your relationship. First, if you score higher than 20, you're still banking on your dad to take care of you financially and to bale you out of your financial scrapes like he did when you were a child. If his score is just as high as yours, then the two of you agree that it's okay for him to be your piggy bank and your instant cash machine. You two probably don't disagree very often about financial issues. Still, your financial arrangement has a down side that you may not have realized yet, as we'll soon discuss. Second, if you score above 20 but he scores more than 5 points lower than you, there's probably a lot of tension between you two over your future plans, your present situation, and your financial decisions. He wants you to be a financial grown-up, and you're still behaving like a little girl. The greater the difference in your two scores, the greater the tension. Third, if you score less than 10 but he scores more than 20, you want to be financially self-reliant, but he wants you to continue depending on him for money. Maybe he feels you won't need him for anything any more once you're on your own financially. Or maybe he's afraid that he won't be able to influence your decisions any more now that you are refusing to take his money to bale you out of whatever might go wrong. Fourth, if both of you score somewhere between 15 and 25 points, you are still having trouble deciding what your financial relationship with each other ought to be—and that detracts from your relationship. In terms of what's best for your father-daughter relationship, the best combination is when both you and your father score less than 10. This means both of you are glad that you are financially self-reliant. Although you may turn to him for advice when you're in a financial jam, you won't expect him to give you money—and he won't feel that the loving thing to do is to give you money. But since many daughters and fathers aren't in this group, let's see how financial issues often detract from your relationship.

Let's start with this "golden rule": "Those who have the gold make the rules." When you accept the "gold" from your father, there are usually strings attached—strings that may be invisible at first but eventually become heavy ropes around both your necks. For instance, you may consider the money your father has given you a gift, but he considers it a loan—money that you're supposed to repay. Other times you both agree that it is a loan, but it's not made clear *when* you're supposed to repay him. At some later date he may feel taken advantage of because you haven't repaid a dime when you clearly have the money. You also can end up resenting your father for giving or loaning money to one of your siblings. But the biggest risks involve obligation and entitlement. Depending on how much of his money you've accepted, you may feel obligated to do things you don't want to do—little things like spending time with him when you really don't want to or big things like going into a career you have absolutely no interest in because he footed the entire bill for your very expensive education. While you're feeling obligated, he's feeling entitled—entitled to have a say in how his money is spent: what school you should attend, what jobs you should apply for, or what investments you should make. Let's be fair to our fathers here: Most of us speak up—and loudly—when someone is using our hard-earned money in ways we don't approve of, right? Both you and your father risk damaging your relationship when you ignore this advice: Don't mix business with pleasure.

Another risk of continuing to bank on your father is believing that he's not sacrificing anything at all by continuing to help you out. Daughters who tell themselves this don't feel guilty or indebted to their father because they're convinced that he has "plenty" of money. After all, look at dad's house, cars, clothes, and vacations. Clearly, he has more than "enough." Besides, if my dad keeps giving me money or expensive gifts without my asking him to, then surely this means he's not sacrificing anything, right? Well, maybe—and maybe not. I have no idea what any father's financial situation actually is, but what I do know for certain is this: Most daughters assume their father isn't sacrificing anything *without knowing* what their father's financial situation actually is. Even at your age, you might not know how much money is left over after your father pays for taxes, health, car and house insurance, house and car payments, medical bills, loans for your college education, or expenses for his elderly parents. If he's hoping to retire at age 65, does he have enough saved to take care of himself and your mother until they die—and to cover nursing home care? (Most men live to age 80, and most women live to age 85.) Is the money he keeps spending on you money he could be using to pay off the mortgage, to retire sooner from a stressful job, or to buy or do something special for himself or your mother? My point isn't to make you feel guilty. My point is that you may not see the sacrifices your father makes by remaining financially tied to you. You may be telling yourself that it's okay because he's doing this freely, voluntarily, and happily. Remember, though, in our country most men are raised to believe that one of the most loving things a father can do is to give money and gifts to his children—and to show this same kind of "love" to his children's children as well (hence the bumper stickers on some older parents' expensive cars or boats: "I don't care what you think, I'm spending my children's inheritance").

Even in the final years of your father's life, banking on him can have a negative impact on your relationship. Woody Allen jokes: "One good thing about being poor is that when you're seventy your children won't have you declared legally insane in order to get control of your estate." But inheritance is no laughing matter. Imagine how you might feel in these situations: Your dad is going to leave all his money to charity. But because you figured you'd be getting an inheritance, you've lived your life spending almost all your income and saving almost nothing for your old age. Or imagine that your dad has planned to leave most of his money to your stepmother and their daughter. Or what if you're the dutiful daughter who has helped your dad run his business, clean his house, and take care of his medical problems for years, whereas your sister has been off somewhere having a grand time doing who knows what—no help and no word from her. As your dad approaches death, guess who shows up—your sister. Overjoyed by her return, your dad announces that he's leaving half his large estate to her and half to you. How does that grab you? (Yes, it's adapted from the "Prodigal Son" biblical story.) Because situations such as these do happen and do tear families apart, I urge you to protect your father-daughter relationship by having open, honest family discussions *now* about everyone's concerns and about inheritance decisions.

Eye Openers

- Children make most long-distance calls on Mother's Day and most *collect* calls on Father's Day.[31]
- Most parents cannot afford to retire at age 65 and are not saving enough money to support themselves in their final years.[23]
- American parents have loaned their adult children about 68 *billion* dollars, although many of their children do not intend to repay the money.[32]
- Most fathers who are millionaires did not inherit their money— they earned it.[33]

So Now What?

Again, I can't tell you what kind of financial relationship you and your father should have. All I can do is point out the negative impact that certain kinds of decisions and attitudes may have on your relationship. I also can point out that many daughters complain that their fathers still treat them like little girls. Yet, when I question them further, it almost always turns out that these daughters are still behaving like little girls in certain ways—relying on daddy's money, bouncing checks, running up big credit-card debts, not paying their bills on time, not planning ahead for the future, and then getting mad at their father whenever he asks questions about their future plans or tries to help them resolve these problems. How can we expect our fathers to treat us like women if we still have our hands out for money like little girls? How can we expect them to respect our judgment if we're still relying on them as our backup bankers or if we're still not able to manage our own money? How can we have an adult relationship if we are still expecting or allowing our fathers to be the big floppy wallet with money flying out of it or an instant cash machine?

As daughters, we have to be honest with ourselves in confronting some tough questions: At what age will we consider ourselves financially grown up? Even if our fathers are willing to keep helping us out, what will it take for us to decide that we want a relationship that is completely separate from daddy's money?If we decide to continue accepting our father's financial help, then when will we stop blaming him for any tensions that might arise over these financial matters? Regardless of what you decide, you *are* banking on yourself to determine the impact that money is going to have on your father-daughter relationship.

Chapter 3

Communication
Open Ears, Open Heart, Open Mind

- Have you ever wished you and your father could talk more comfortably?

- Do you ever feel tense or intimidated when you disagree or argue with your father?

- Do you ever feel that your father isn't listening to you or doesn't understand what you're feeling?

- Do you think your father gives you too much advice or lectures you too much?

- Do you have a hard time understanding each other's point of view?

If you find yourself answering yes to these questions, then this chapter will strengthen your relationship with your father by teaching you how to communicate more effectively. Let's begin by using the following quiz to assess how you and your father communicate. If you're comfortable enough, ask your father to take the quiz too, and then talk about your answers together.

If your scores are above 40, you're expert communicators. But if your scores are below 20, your styles of communicating are working against your relationship. Scores between 20 and 40 mean that there are certain skills you or your dad need to learn that can strengthen your relationship.

Emotional Intelligence

The skills listed in the following quiz are sometimes referred to as *emotional intelligence*.[1] Emotional intelligence means being able to initiate conversations,

How Emotionally Intelligent Are You and Your Father?[1]

How do you and your father communicate with each other? In addressing the following statements, use 0 to mean "never," 1 to mean "rarely," 2 to mean "usually," and 3 to mean "almost always."

You Dad

____ ____ Your father expresses feelings openly and comfortably.

____ ____ Your father recognizes what others are feeling.

____ ____ Your father expresses anger in an appropriate way.

____ ____ Your father expresses sympathy and concern for others.

____ ____ Your father resolves conflicts by talking them through.

____ ____ Your father feels comfortable when others express their feelings.

____ ____ Your father allows others to talk without constantly interrupting or dominating the conversation.

____ ____ Your father expresses opinions without insulting the other person.

____ ____ Your father pays attention to what others are saying.

____ ____ Your father interprets others' nonverbal messages and feelings accurately.

____ ____ Your father maintains eye contact and looks relaxed in conversations.

____ ____ Your father joins in and carries on conversations.

____ ____ Your father accepts negative feedback without getting angry or defensive.

____ ____ Your father recognizes and controls his own emotions rather than being overwhelmed by them.

____ ____ Your father draws people into conversations and makes them feel comfortable.

____ ____ Your scores (45 possible)

talk comfortably about personal matters, read other people's feelings from their expressions, be in touch with what you are feeling, put other people at ease in a conversation, and keep a conversation going. Odds are that your emotional intelligence score is higher than your father's—but not because you were born with special skills or because you have a more communicative personality than your dad. Your score is probably higher because, from early childhood on, we females are trained to behave in these ways and are given years of practice to develop these particular skills. Sadly, most boys are denied this same level of training and practice, leaving most men with less emotional intelligence than most women by time they become husbands or fathers.[2] Again though, this does not mean that females are "naturally" better communicators than males or that your personalities cause you and your dad to communicate the way you do.

Think of you and your father this way: One morning you wake up on another planet. You're afraid, confused, and sad. You desperately want to get back to Earth. Luckily, the beings on this planet speak English—and they're friendly. But every time you try to tell them how afraid you are or ask them for advice about getting back to Earth, they stop talking and start tapping on the top of your head. When you start to cry, they get even stranger: They all run away. You interpret this to mean that these beings have no empathy or intelligence. Too bad you didn't read the interplanetary communication handbook, which explained that on this planet the inhabitants are taught to express love by patting one another on the head and not talking. On this planet crying means that you're angry and ready to attack. Both you and the friendly creatures have miscommunicated. And there you are, stranded and miserable. And there they are, confused and frightened.

Because you and your father have been taught to communicate differently, you sometimes misjudge and misinterpret one another. For example, if you have never seen your father cry or express sadness publicly, you may wrongly assume that he isn't sensitive, compassionate, or tender hearted. Or if he doesn't start conversations or ask questions about personal or emotional things, you may jump to the conclusion that he isn't interested in what's going on in your life and has nothing worth sharing that might help you with your emotional struggles or relationships.

What's happening is that you're interpreting and judging his behavior as if he were a woman. You're using the female communication handbook. He's using the male handbook. Your female way of communicating is not necessarily any better than his male way. We can be judgmental and condescending by insisting that men learn to communicate and to express their emotions in exactly the same ways we women have been taught to do. Or we can take a kinder, quicker approach and learn to recognize and interpret the differences between male and female styles so we won't misinterpret and misjudge as often. The following quiz and the "Eye Openers" that follow give you a closer look at how males and females communicate.

Are You and Your Dad from Different Planets?

Check the statements that you believe are true for most men in our country.

____ Males complain more than females.

____ Males are more likely than females to talk about problems in their relationships.

____ Males tend to lash out and females tend to retreat into silence when they are angry.

____ Males dominate conversations and talk more than females do.

____ Males are not as easily hurt as females are by what people say or do to them.

____ Males are more comfortable than females arguing with people they love.

____ Males are less intimidated by angry females than females are by angry males.

____ Males get angry faster and more often than females.

____ Males criticize and ridicule people more often than females.

____ Males are less sympathetic and less compassionate than females.

____ Score (10 possible)

Eye Openers

- With permission and practice, males are just as communicative as females.[2,8]
- Some well-educated fathers with high-paying jobs sign up for workshops to learn how to communicate better with their children.[9]
- Middle-aged fathers tend to communicate with their children better than younger fathers.[10,11]

If your score is higher than 5, you're making a number of negative assumptions about men—assumptions that probably make it harder for you and your father to communicate. As you learned in Chapter 1, your beliefs and expectations—even when they are not based on fact—influence the way you treat your father. This is why it is so crucial that you realize that *not one of the statements in the quiz is true.* Most men in our country do not behave in the ways described in the quiz.[1-7] Now go back and reread the quiz; but this time remember that every statement is false. So ask yourself: How might my relationship with my father have been different if I had realized these things about how men communicate while I was growing up?

Your Power, Your Father's Fears

Power—what does the word mean? When I'm talking about communication, by power I mean being able to get your feelings and ideas across in a way that is most likely to get what you want from the other person. For instance, let's say you want to let your father know how angry you are at him, and you want an apology from him. You might communicate by crying and speaking in a fragile "little girl" tone. Because your dad is undone whenever he sees you cry, he quickly gives you what you want—an apology. You weren't communicating in a mature way, but you definitely had the power.

By this definition of power, there are three ways in which most women have more power than most men. First, because you're a woman, you've had more instruction and more practice in emotional intelligence skills. And the most emotionally intelligent person has the upper hand (more power) in communicating..

Second, women's ways of communicating are often more powerful than men's because we tend to engage in more passive-aggressive behavior and more "emotional blackmail."[12] We get the other person to do what we want because we're more apt than he is to pout, cry, walk out, hang up, throw a tantrum, make him feel guilty, or act like the helpless victim in order to make him pity us. We use passive-aggressive ways to express ourselves—give him the cold shoulder, ignore him, say mean things about him behind his back, or exclude him. As a woman, your ways of communicating are probably more emotionally threatening to your father than his are to you. In short, you have the most power. [12,13]

Third, you have more power because our society publicly mocks and criticizes men more than women for the way they communicate. This means your father starts out with a disadvantage because he's been told that his male style of communicating is inferior to your female style. Greeting cards, advertisements, TV shows, movies, cartoons, and magazine articles often criticize the way men communicate in ways that would infuriate women if the tables were turned. Consider greeting cards that insult men in these ways: A guilty-looking boy on the front of the card says that apologizing isn't easy but that being stupid is—and he asks for forgiveness. (You will have a hard time finding a similar apology card for women to give to men.) Another card lists the ingredients in a man: vanity, self-centeredness, arrogance, insensitivity, thoughtlessness, insincerity, the communication skills of a chimp, and an ego the size of a landfill. These are only a couple of the examples that Warren Farrell, an expert on male-female relationships, offers to demonstrate how men are publicly humiliated and ridiculed for the ways they communicate.[4]

Of course we need to have a sense of humor—to make fun of ourselves and others in greeting cards, jokes, and advertisements. Still, we ridicule men publicly for being lousy communicators far more than we ridicule any other group of people. Through humor, we often fuel the belief that *because your father is male*, he doesn't have the feelings, the sensitivities, the skills, or the desire to communicate like you do *because you're female*.

Helping Your Father Feel Safe

When we don't feel safe in conversations, we say and do things that work against good communication. Especially when a conversation is "crucial," we tend to feel unsafe—insecure, frightened, foolish, or defensive. A *crucial* conversation is one in which the stakes are high because the outcome probably will have an impact on the relationship. We feel vulnerable because we're afraid that something bad is going to happen if we speak honestly or share our feelings. This is when we do our worst communicating. Use the following checklist to see how you and your dad behave when either of you feel insecure or unsafe.[14]

How Dad and I Behave in Crucial Conversations

How do your father and you generally behave when you're having a crucial conversation? In addressing the following issues, use 0 to mean "never," 1 to mean "rarely," 2 to mean "half the time," and 3 to mean "often."

You Dad

___ ___ Clamming up

___ ___ Only giving short answers

___ ___ Joking or laughing at a serious comment

___ ___ Making insulting or sarcastic remarks

___ ___ Walking away

___ ___ Hanging up

___ ___ Changing the subject

___ ___ Exaggerating in order to make a point

___ ___ Yelling or cursing

___ ___ Sidestepping or avoiding questions

___ ___ Looking or sounding bored or uninterested

___ ___ Name calling

(Continued)

___ ___ Crying or pouting

___ ___ Making "all or nothing" comments such as *never, all, always, everyone*

___ ___ Labeling each other such as *you men* or *you women*

___ ___ Denying that you are upset when you are

___ ___ Interrupting a lot

___ ___ Talking louder or faster

___ ___ Attacking the other's intelligence

___ ___ Acting as if the topic is trivial and unimportant

___ ___ Scores (60 possible)

The higher your scores, the more difficult it is for you and your father to carry on a crucial conversation. And the higher your scores, the more each of you needs to do things that will make the other person feel safe and more secure. The next quiz offers you ideas for how you can have better crucial conversations with your father.[14]

Most of us feel more secure and safe when the other person reassures us at the outset that they aren't going to punish us somehow for what we say. In your father's case, he may be afraid that you're going to punish him by making fun of what he says, by bursting into tears, or by withdrawing emotionally. Like you, he doesn't want to look foolish or stupid. If you want him to be honest, open, and comfortable talking with you—especially about really touchy subjects—you can say reassuring things such as, "Dad, I'm not going to love you any less if you tell me truthfully what happened" or "I'm not going to make fun of you if you tell me how you feel."

Advice or Interference

If you're like most of us, you feel more insecure and more defensive when someone is giving you advice—especially when that someone is your parent. When your father is offering advice, how do you usually feel? Hopefully, you feel loved, comforted, relaxed, and grateful. You feel that he's treating

How Safe Do I Help Dad Feel?

Check each of these things you usually do when you are having an important or emotional conversation with your father.

_____ Talk in private so that nobody else can interfere or interrupt

_____ Talk when neither of you is tired, grumpy, or preoccupied

_____ Encourage him to keep talking by saying such things as, "Tell me more" and "What else?"

_____ Find things that you agree on and state them, such as, "I'm glad we both agree that . . ."

_____ Use the word *and* instead of *but* as often as you can, such as, "We disagree about this *and* that's why"

_____ Find a shared goal and state it, such as, "We both want to come up with a good solution for this"

_____ Reassure him that you're not out to hurt, punish, blame, or humiliate him

_____ Don't state your opinions as if they were facts

_____ Find something to compliment in what he says

_____ Avoid judgmental words, such as, "How stupid!"

_____ Your score (10 possible)

you like an equal and is advising you because he loves you. Unfortunately, though, even as older women we may feel tense, hurt, or annoyed when dad starts giving us advice. We feel that he's interfering, lecturing, or treating us like a little girl. Here are eight ideas to keep in mind whenever you feel yourself getting annoyed at your father for giving advice.

1. Remember That Men and Women Are Taught to Give Advice Differently

Generally, we females are taught to give advice only *after* we have reassured the other person that we have "heard" and empathized with their feelings.

First, we spend lots of time talking about how the other person feels. Then we often share a story about something similar that has happened to us that means, "I understand just how you feel." After that, we gently offer advice in a carefully worded, tentative way: "Do you think it might help if . . .," "One thing I did when I was in a situation like yours was . . . ," or "I'm not sure this would work, but you might want to. . . ." In contrast, most males are taught that the best way to nurture and to help someone is to jump right in and offer advice on how to fix whatever is wrong—whether it's a broken heart or a broken car. Instead of dwelling a lot on how you feel or expressing a lot of sympathy for you, your dad immediately starts offering you ideas for "fixing it." Because he wants you to feel better as quickly as possible, he immediately starts offering you advice in a way that is more direct and more blunt than most women probably would. In turn, you misinterpret this to mean that he isn't interested in how you're feeling or isn't sympathetic enough.

2. Focus on His Motives, Not His Style

Stop focusing on the particular words or style your father uses. Focus instead on his motives and his feelings. Who is he trying to help? What is he feeling? If you focus on this, you'll probably see that he's not angry or disappointed—he's worried and frustrated. He's afraid because whatever has upset or hurt you might happen again, maybe with worse consequences for you next time. He's frustrated because he knows that he isn't going to be able to protect you or solve most of the problems in your life. Get it? He's feeling frustrated or afraid *for you, not for himself.* Just keep reminding yourself: My father is *not* trying to judge or to scold me. He is trying to nurture and to protect me.

3. Figure Out Who Is Really Judging You

When you're upset with your father for giving you advice, ask yourself whose judgment you're actually reacting to—yours or his? Often the voice inside your head saying "You screwed up" or "Shame on you" is yours, not his. Even though you may feel that it's your father who is judging you, often you are judging yourself. You may feel ashamed because you know that this particular problem or situation *is* your fault. Or you may feel embarrassed because your father warned you ahead of time about this particular thing and you ignored his advice. Or even at your age, you may feel you have to prove to your father that you're a competent, intelligent person who doesn't need any advice from him. In other words, when you feel foolish, incompetent, or ashamed of yourself, you're going to feel criticized or judged by your father, no matter how lovingly or gently he offers his advice.

4. *Tell Him What You're Feeling*

If his advice starts to upset you, tell him. You might say something like: "I'm getting the feeling that you think I'm an idiot. It sure would help right now to hear that you think I'm basically doing a pretty good job handling things" or "I'm feeling like you're angry or disappointed in me. And that makes me feel even worse" or "The way you're talking to me, I get the feeling that I'm a huge embarrassment to you." When daughters use this approach, they are surprised to hear their fathers say such things as: "I'm not mad at you. I'm just scared that worse things will happen to you if you don't follow some of my advice" or "It's not that I think you're stupid. It's just that I learned the hard way about this sort of thing and I don't want to see you get hurt the way I did."

5. *Put Yourself in His Place*

Consider how you behave when you're in your father's place—the person giving (or wanting to give) advice to someone you care about. Haven't you ever been accused of interfering or being judgmental when all you were trying to do was spare that person some pain? Haven't you sometimes felt torn about whether to give someone advice because you were afraid of how he or she would react, yet you desperately wanted to help? And isn't it hard for you to give someone lots of sympathy when they have repeatedly ignored the advice you've offered them? Before you get too irritated with your father, remember how difficult it has been for you at times when you've been in his situation as the advice giver.

6. Ask Him About His Difficult Experiences

Before you tell your dad about a situation that's upsetting you or before asking for his advice, start with this: "Dad, I'd like to know if you've ever been in a situation like the one I'm going to tell you about. Before you talk to me about my problem, would you tell me about the situation you were in? How was your situation like mine? How was it different? How did you feel? What did you do? Who did you go to for advice? How did you react to their advice? Who were you afraid to go to for advice, and why?" Get your father to talk about the times he felt like you're feeling now *before* you give him lots of details about your own situation.

Why am I urging you to do this? Because when he tells you about his mistakes, you probably won't be as defensive when he gives you advice. You'll probably be more open to his advice knowing that he's been through something like you're going through. And you'll probably see that his motive is not to judge or control you but to spare you from going through something bad or sad like he did. By getting your father to tell you his own story first, he gets a chance to give you advice in a way you're more comfortable with. By the way, every daughter I know who has tried this says that it brought her and her father closer.

7. Tell Him Whether You Want Sympathy, Approval, or Advice

Before you start complaining or telling him what's upsetting you, tell your dad what it is you want from him: sympathy, approval, or advice. You really need to do this. Remember, most males have been taught that the best way to comfort someone is to help them fix whatever is bothering them. So if all you want is sympathy—a listener who basically says "You poor thing"— then let your father know. You can do this by saying such things as: "Dad, I'm really upset, and I want to tell you about it. I just need your shoulder to cry on for an hour or so before you give me any advice" or "I need your sympathy. I'm not ready quite yet to try to work on ways to fix this mess." I've found that daughters are often after their father's approval—not his advice. The well-meaning father gives her what he thinks she wants—his help. Then the daughter ends up annoyed because dad didn't give her what she really wanted—his approval.

To help you decide whether it's advice or approval you want in any particular situation, ask yourself if you're going to be hurt or annoyed if your father does any of these things: points out the weaknesses in your ideas, tells you where he thinks you went wrong, comes up with better ideas than yours, helps you see how you could have done things better, asks you questions about things you haven't thought through carefully, or explains why certain things you're saying aren't accurate or can't possibly work? If your answer is yes, then what you really want is his approval, not his advice. When it's approval you want from your father, you want him to say whatever it takes to make you feel good—even if he has to lie or keep quiet. And if he's giving advice when you're wanting approval, then you end up saying things to him like: "You're always dumping on my ideas," "You're so critical," "You're always trying to tell me what to do," or "You don't think I do anything right, do you?"

You also might think about advice and approval this way: If you're thrashing around in the water with a blindfold over your eyes and you're drowning—too far from shore for your father to swim out to rescue you—what response do you want from him? *Approval:* "You're doing a great job!" *Sympathy:* "Oh, you poor thing." Or *advice:* "Stop thrashing around like that, take off your blindfold, and grab the life jacket floating beside you." I doubt that you'll make it to shore if your dad only gives you sympathy or approval. But if you follow his advice, once you're ashore, I sure hope that you don't accuse him of being judgmental or trying to tell you how to run your life. On the other hand, I hope your dad has the good sense not to stand there yelling at you while you're drowning: "I told you to wear a life jacket! If only you had followed my advice!"

8. *Thank Him*

When your father gives you advice in a way you really like, thank him. Then thank him again a day or so later. You might say such things as: "I can't tell you how much it meant to me yesterday when you sat there just listening to me talk about my feelings," "I feel so close to you when you

Eye Openers[15–18]

- Fathers are usually more direct and more blunt than mothers in telling their children things they don't want to admit about themselves.
- Fathers are more likely than mothers to talk with children about how to solve problems and how to become more self-reliant.
- Fathers are less likely than mothers to let children whine, complain, or feel sorry for themselves instead of trying to solve the problem.

tell me about times you've made mistakes like mine," or "You really made me feel better by asking me all these questions about how I'm feeling." *Warning:* When you compliment him, don't do it in a critical way by saying such things as: "Thanks for not lecturing me *like you usually do*" or "I appreciate your listening to me *for a change.*"

Dealing with Anger

Anyone can become angry—that is easy. But to be angry with the right person, to the right degree, at the right time, for the right purpose, and in the right way—this is not easy.

ARISTOTLE

How do you react when you're mad at your father or when he's mad at you? Are you usually able to get your feelings out in the open and resolve things? Or do you pout, yell, shut down, clam up, or go to someone else to complain about him?

Why is anger often so difficult for fathers and daughters to deal with? In part, it's because males and females are taught to express anger and to react to other people's anger in such different ways. Men are usually taught that it's not okay to express their anger at women—only at other men. If he's mad at a woman, he's supposed to tell her what's wrong as calmly as he can, wait for his anger to go away on its own, or do something athletic to work off his anger—go jogging or play basketball. We women, on the other hand, are usually taught that it *is* okay to let people know that we're mad at them—regardless of whether they're male or female. Unlike men, we're taught to express our anger in more indirect, passive-aggressive ways, such as crying, pouting, withdrawing affection, excluding or ignoring the other person, giving them the cold shoulder or the silent treatment, throwing a temper tantrum, walking away, hanging up, acting sad or depressed, or responding with "If you can't figure out why I'm mad at you, I'm not going to tell you."[1,20]

How do these differences between men and women cause problems for you and your father? First, it probably takes him a lot longer to figure out that you're mad at him—and to figure out *why* you're mad—than it takes you to figure out why he's mad at you. Second, your ways of expressing anger may be more painful and more difficult for him to deal with because they're more indirect and more emotionally manipulative than his. So the next time you and your dad are upset with each other, follow this four-step approach:

1. Remember, You Were Both Taught to React This Way

Keep telling yourself: "This is the way my father and I have been *taught* to deal with anger. This isn't something permanent or inborn in either of us. I can learn better ways to express my anger." While you're learning new ways to express your anger, you're likely to feel uncomfortable—maybe even a little afraid—because it's new to you. That's okay. The more you practice expressing your anger in new ways, the more natural it will feel.

2. Step Outside the Situation

Use the following quiz to look at how you and your father each deal with anger. Think about how you feel and what you gain or lose when you behave the way you usually do. The goal is to change your behavior, not his. And when you change, odds are that you will get a better response from him.

If you and your dad score above 30, your way of expressing anger creates a lot of stress for both of you. If your scores are under 10, you two are

---

Volcanoes: Handling Anger

When you and your father are angry with one another, how do you usually behave? In addressing the following issues, use 0 to mean "never," 1 to mean "rarely," 2 to mean "half the time," and 3 to mean "almost always."

Dad   Me

___ ___ Clams up or refuses to talk any more about it

___ ___ Pouts

___ ___ Yells

___ ___ Leaves the room or hangs up

___ ___ Drinks too much

___ ___ Turns on music or TV for distraction

___ ___ Withdraws emotionally (the silent treatment, the cold shoulder)

___ ___ Curses

___ ___ Says hurtful things

___ ___ Cries or resorts to a very pitiful tone of voice

___ ___ Complains to someone else instead of working it out together

___ ___ Threatens to do something that would hurt the other emotionally

___ ___ Total score (36 possible)

---

usually able to get your feelings out in the open and to work out your problems without damaging your relationship.

3. *Don't Go Behind His Back*

Stop going to other people behind his back when you're mad at your dad. Go to him. Put yourself in his place: How do you feel when someone goes behind your back instead of telling you why they're upset with you? If it's hard for you to express anger to your father directly, odds are you're afraid of something. The first thing you need to do is tell him why you're afraid. Don't start by talking to him about why you're mad at him. That comes later. Start out by telling him why you're usually too tense or afraid to express your anger directly to him. What are you afraid he's going to say or do? Are you afraid that you will lose something if you tell him how you feel—lose his love or lose his money? Are you afraid he will get so angry that it will permanently damage your relationship? Whatever it is that scares you, tell him. You might say something like: "Dad, I'm going to talk to you about why I'm mad instead of clamming up or pouting like I usually do. But I'm afraid that telling you why I'm mad will damage our relationship." Or say: "I'm afraid to talk to you about how angry I am because you might start yelling at me. I want to get to the point where I'm not afraid to tell you when I'm angry at you. I want to stop talking to people about it behind your back. But I'm afraid you will drink too much if I tell you what I'm mad about."

4. Ask Him to Tell You an Anger Story

Ask your father to tell you stories about times when he's been angry at people and when people have been angry at him. Choose a time when you and he are *alone* and relaxed, not when you're angry at each other. Use the questions in the next box to keep the conversation rolling. My bet is that if you get your father to tell you stories about anger in his own life, you'll be less afraid to tell him when you're angry at him and less upset when he gets angry at you. Just give it a try. I guarantee you this: You're going to hear some interesting stories and learn things about your father that will probably surprise you.

Emotional Blackmail

Have you ever left a conversation feeling that you were somehow tricked into saying or doing something you really didn't want to? Do you wonder how the person managed to manipulate you? In many cases you've been the victim of a manipulative style of communicating referred to as *emotional blackmail.*[12]

Anger: Questions for My Father

Ask your father to tell you a story about a time when he was angry with someone. As he talks, ask him:

1. How did you let the person know you were angry?
2. What impact did it have on your relationship?
3. What were you most worried about when you let the person know that you were angry?
4. How did the person respond?
5. What do you wish you had done differently?
6. When the person got angry at you, how did it affect you?
7. What's the best way for someone to let you know that they're mad at you?
8. What's hardest for you when someone is mad at you?
9. What's hard for you in expressing your anger?
10. What lessons have you learned about getting angry or dealing with others' anger?
11. As you were growing up, how did each person in your family deal with conflict?
12. How was anger handled and expressed in your family?

When someone is threatening to stop loving you or is punishing you emotionally when you won't do what they want, that's emotional blackmail. Because these people know you so well, and because you care about them or want their approval, they know where you're most vulnerable. Emotional blackmailers threaten to deprive you of those things they know you want the most. They get you to do what they want by surrounding you with FOG—Fear, Obligation, and Guilt.[12] They try to make you feel afraid by threatening to withdraw something that they control—love, public approval, money, promotions, and so on. Emotional blackmailers try to make you feel obligated or indebted to them—to feel that you owe them something in return for whatever it is they have done for you. They try to make you feel guilty by implying that you're not loving, loyal, kind, or good enough. An emotional blackmailer often says such things as: "How could you do this to me after all I've done for you? Why are you ruining my life? Can't you see how much you're hurting me? How can you embarrass me like this? I wouldn't feel so depressed if it wasn't for what you're doing. You're so selfish and disloyal."

The best emotional blackmailers make it nearly impossible to recognize what they're doing while they're doing it. It may take days or even years for you to figure out that you are being manipulated by the way they are communicating with you. It's also hard to recognize what they're doing because when we give them what they want, they shower us with the goodies— love, praise, approval, attention, promotions, gifts, or money. And that feels good. Ironically, one of the most powerful ways to manipulate someone is to act weak, powerless, and fragile. Think back to the times that you've gotten your father to give in to you because you made him feel sorry for you by crying, acting pathetic, or using a childlike, pitiful tone of voice. You had power over him by acting weak. Also think back to the times when your father got you to do what he wanted by making you feel sorry for him. Both you and your father probably use emotional blackmail against each other at times. But you and the other women in your family probably do most of the emotional blackmailing because men usually are taught to communicate in more direct, less manipulative ways than women.

Whether it is you or your father who is being blackmailed, what can the other person do? First, the person being blackmailed needs to get clear on what's happening by asking himself or herself: (1) Exactly what is it that the other person wants me to do?[12] (2) What emotional weapons is this person using—fear, obligation, or guilt? (3) How does he or she respond when I don't agree to do what he or she wants—cry, yell, withdraw, give me "the look," or threaten to take something away from me? (4) What is he or she trying to get me to feel—afraid, guilty, selfish, disloyal, or ungrateful? (5) What belief of mine makes it so easy for this person to blackmail me—that it's my duty to make him or her happy, that I'm obligated to do what this person wants because I owe him or her something, or that love means always giving the other person what he or she wants?

Second, state out loud what's going on and how it makes you feel. For example, your father can say such things to you as: "I feel angry because I feel that you're trying to overpower and manipulate me by crying" or "I feel hurt because you seem to be suggesting that I'm not a generous man because I won't buy this particular thing for you." Or you might say to him: "Dad, I'm angry because I feel that you're trying to get me to do what you want by using religion to make me feel guilty" or "I feel insulted because you seem to be bribing me with money to get me to give in to you on this."

Third, tell emotional blackmailers that their emotional weapons aren't going to work this time. At the same time, reassure emotional blackmailers that they have a right to their feelings and opinions. When someone is pressuring us to do what they want, we tend to get into long discussions in which we get angrier as we both defend our positions. The more the other person refuses to budge, the more aggressive and defensive we usually get. It's like the contest between the sun and the wind to see which one can make the person take off his or her coat. The wind angrily huffs and puffs, trying to blow the person's coat off, but the person keeps tightening his or her grip on the coat. The sun calmly and patiently keeps shining, and the person finally gets so warm that he or she happily takes off the coat.

If you and your father just can't agree or can't find a solution to a problem, don't keep huffing and puffing like the wind. After you've each had the chance to express yourselves, and once you realize that continuing to talk is just getting nowhere, you need to bring the conversation to an end. You can saying such things as: "I feel bad that you're still upset with me and that we can't find a solution that satisfies both of us, but I'm not changing my mind about this particular thing," "I can understand why you see things that way; but I'm not going to agree to do what you're asking," "That's an interesting point, but I've already made my choice," "In the past I was so afraid of losing your respect that I always said yes to you, but I'm not going to agree anymore to do things that I truly believe are bad for me," "There are no bad guys here, so we'll just have to agree to disagree about this," or "I know you're hurt; but I can't do something that I don't believe in just to make you happy. And this situation isn't something I can compromise on."

Finally—and most important—you need to make clear to your father that your relationship does not have to be hurt just because the two of you can't agree or can't compromise on a particular issue or decision. You can say such things as: "Dad, I'm going ahead with my plans even though you disapprove. And it's up to you whether you let us drift apart because of this" or "I know you're really disappointed with my decision. When you've had more time to think about it, maybe you'll feel differently. But either way, we can both agree that our relationship is too important to let this come between us."

The worst response is to cave in to the emotional blackmailer's demands. Giving in guarantees that they will use the same manipulative methods again because they got what they wanted. For instance, if you cry and pout when you're trying to get your way, your father shouldn't surrender just because he feels sorry for you. It might even be a good idea if he told you that until you're ready to communicate more maturely, he isn't going to allow you to keep beating him up emotionally. And you should do the same when your father is using emotional weapons against you. It is best for your relationship if you don't use fear, obligation, and guilt to get your way.

Asking Your Father to Change

If you want to ask your father to change some aspect of his behavior, here's a three-step method that has worked for most daughters I have counseled:

1. *Make just one request.* When you're talking with your father about something that you wish was different in your relationship, only discuss one thing at a time. For example, if you'd like to talk to your father about paying more attention to you, stick to that one topic. Don't bring up the other five things you'd like changed. When we stuff too many issues or complaints into one conversation, the other person tends to feel overwhelmed and attacked.

2. *Be specific.* Choose words that are specific enough so that your father knows exactly what it is you want him to do differently. When we're asking someone to change something about themselves, we tend to use words that are vague and confusing—words that mean one thing to you and something else altogether to the other person. For example, when you say, "I want my father to pay more attention to me," you might mean, "I want him to look at me when I'm talking to him," or you might mean, "I want him to ask me more questions about what's going on in my life." Or if you say to your dad, "Don't embarrass me," you might mean "Don't curse around my friends," or you might mean, "Don't drink too much the next time you're at my place." You can practice

wording things in precise, specific terms by doing the exercises in the following box.

3. *Tell him how you feel.* If something your father says or does upsets you, start out by telling him how it makes you feel, not by telling him what you want him to change. Talking about your feelings helps your father to understand why you'd like him to change the way he's doing something. Unlike opinions or ideas, our feelings aren't something that the other person can argue with us about. You and your dad can disagree about whose beliefs are right or wrong—or whose facts about a particular matter are not correct—but you can't argue with each other about what either of you feels. A feeling can't be right or wrong. It's simply a feeling. So here are some ways to start conversations with the focus on feelings: "I feel sad when you only talk to me about my work." "I'd feel closer to you if you asked about my personal and spiritual life." "I feel lonely and sad when you ask my brother to do things alone with you, but you never ask me to go anywhere alone with you." "I feel unimportant when you keep watching TV or reading the paper while I'm trying to talk to you."

Asking Dad to Change: What Do I Mean?

Word these statements in a more specific, precise way:

"Listen to me, dad."

"Stop treating me like a child."

"Don't be so condescending and insulting."

"I want you to respect my opinions."

"Don't put me on a guilt trip."

"Don't embarrass me again."

"Why do you have to be so uptight?"

"I want you to trust me."

"Stop pushing me around."

Is It Worth It?

If you decide to use the ideas in this chapter, will it be worth it? Here's what many daughters say:

Angela: "Since I've stopped assuming I know how dad feels without asking him first, things have improved beyond what I ever expected."

Anne: "Now that I tell my father that I do value his opinions, he's stopped giving me so much advice. I almost want him to give me more."

Britta: "Instead of getting frustrated like I used to when he'd ask me questions, I see now that he asks because he loves me, not because he's trying to pry or interfere with my life."

Tina: "Now that I wait to talk to him until I can see he's feeling more relaxed, our communication is so much better. That's the way I've always treated my boyfriends. So I don't know why I never did it before with my dad."

Lucia: "I've almost stopped pouting and walking away every time we disagree about something. He even complimented me on it a few days ago."

I hope you will share what you've learned about communicating with other daughters as a way of helping them embrace their fathers more openly and honestly. Now let's move on to see how these new ways of communicating can help you and your father get to know one another on a deeper level.

Chapter 4

Who Is This Man?
Drawing Dad Out, Allowing Dad In

- Do you and your mother know one another better than you and your father do?

- Do you or your dad avoid discussing your personal values or your lifestyles?

- Are you and your dad uncomfortable talking on a personal level with no one else around?

- Are there things you would like to discuss with him, but you don't know how?

If so, you may be like the little girl who asks, "How can Tarzan have been so smart, so strong, and so magnificent that without help from anyone at all he defeated every one of the jungle animals, including the mighty lion?" The listener replied, "Child, you'll get a different story if the lion learns to talk." Like the lion, your father has his own versions of reality and his own feelings about things that have affected his life and yours. So instead of relying on what others tell you about his life, why not go straight to the lion, so to speak? By learning how to help your "lion" open up more to you and how to help yourself open up more to him, you move your relationship to a more meaningful level. Remember, too: You don't have unlimited time to get to know your "lion."

Before going any further, use the following checklist to consider how you see your father at the present time. As you put the ideas in this chapter to use in getting to know your father better, return to this checklist and note how some of your perceptions have changed.

Who Do You Think Your Father Is?

In addressing the following issues, use 0 to mean "never," 1 to mean "rarely," 2 to mean "about half the time," and 3 to mean "almost always/extremely."

Positive	*Negative*
___ Hard working	___ Underachiever
___ Confident/assured	___ Low self-esteem
___ Self-reliant	___ Dependent/needy
___ Logical/rational	___ Emotional/irrational
___ Assertive/outspoken	___ Meek/shy
___ Forgiving	___ Unforgiving
___ Nurturing	___ Cold/distant
___ Considerate	___ Inconsiderate/rude
___ Reliable/trustworthy	___ Unreliable/disloyal
___ Unselfish/generous	___ Stingy/greedy
___ Flexible	___ Rigid
___ Reflective/introspective	___ Shallow
___ Frank/straightforward	___ Sneaky/manipulative
___ Fair/reasonable	___ Bossy/domineering
___ Accepting/understanding	___ Demanding/critical
___ Insightful/wise	___ Shallow/superficial
___ Humble	___ Arrogant/boastful
___ Open minded	___ Intolerant/judgmental
___ Approachable	___ Intimidating
___ Religious/spiritual	___ Nonspiritual
___ Relaxed	___ Anxious/tense
___ Contented	___ Dissatisfied/bitter
___ Upbeat/optimistic	___ Depressed/pessimistic

Score ___

Score ___ (69 possible)

If your score is higher than 60 in the positive column, you have a very positive image of your father. There's nothing wrong with that, of course, unless you are unable to recognize his weaknesses and shortcomings. This means that you ought to have some negative traits checked as well. So if your score in the negative column is less than 10, getting to know your father better may help you see him more realistically. On the other hand, if your score in the positive column is less than 25 and in the negative column is more than 50, then you have an extremely negative view of your father. In that case, getting to know your father better can help you understand where some of his negative traits came from and may help you feel a little more compassion for him.

Emotional Intimacy: Knowing versus Loving Someone

Let's start by focusing on the difference between *loving* someone and *knowing* someone. Think of a person you know very well but don't love. Now think of yourself as a young child. You loved your parents. You felt close to them. You got along with them. But you did not really know either of them. You didn't have much of a clue what went on in their day-to-day lives apart from you—and you didn't know much about their pasts. Yet, even at your age, you can love your parents without really knowing them very well—and without them knowing you all that well either.

Sadly, even though most fathers and daughters say that they love each other, most daughters and mothers know one another better. This means that they share more about themselves with each other, talk about more personal issues, and spend more time together without anyone else around. This does not necessarily mean that you and your mom enjoy each other more or get along better than you and your dad do. But if you're like most families, you and your mother know each other far better than you and your father do.[1-6] And that's a loss for both you and your dad.

If you and your father are going to get to know each other better, you have to become more emotionally intimate. Being emotionally intimate means being able to talk comfortably and openly with each other about personal things and about your feelings. Being emotionally intimate does not mean being physically or sexually intimate. It means doing the kinds

Emotional Intimacy

How emotionally intimate is your relationship with each of your parents? In addressing these issues, use 0 to mean "never," 1 to mean "rarely," 2 to mean "about half the time," and 3 to mean "almost always."

Dad Mom

___ ___ Comfortable being ourselves around each other

___ ___ Feel relaxed together when nobody else is around

___ ___ Can express deep sadness around one another

___ ___ Can confide in one another

___ ___ Talk with one another about personal, meaningful things

___ ___ Talk directly to each other instead of needing a go-between

___ ___ Recognize each other's shortcomings instead of pretending they don't exist

___ ___ Enjoy spending time *alone* with each other

___ ___ Feel free to express our honest opinions with each other

___ ___ Disagree or argue with each other comfortably

___ ___ Scores (30 possible)

of things described in the following quiz—things that allow the other person to know you as well as you know him or her. If you're like most daughters, up to this point in your life you have been more emotionally intimate with your mother than with your father—which is a loss for you and for him and which is why too many daughters regret not having gotten to know their father very well while he was still alive.[7–9]

If you scored less than 10, you and your parent do not have an emotionally intimate relationship. This doesn't necessarily mean that you fight or argue a lot. You may get along pretty well most of the time. And it doesn't mean that you don't love each other. Still, you're not emotionally intimate enough to know one another very well. If you're fortunate enough to have scored more than 25 on your father's side, you two do know each other well because you are emotionally intimate. With scores between 11 and 25, there's a lot you can learn from this chapter to help you to know your "lion" and allow him to know you. Let's look at seven steps for opening you and your father up to each other at a more meaningful, more intimate level.

Step 1: Make More Effort

If you want you and your father to know each other better, stop telling yourself, "Well, naturally, my mother and I know each other better and are more intimate—we're both female." Dump that thought. Focus on what we've already learned in the last few chapters: Most males and females are *taught* to communicate differently and *taught* to believe that mothers and daughters are supposed to be more open, more personal, and more involved with each other. The only thing that's "natural" is that you and your father are "naturally" behaving the way you were trained to behave. Now's your chance to learn to relate more meaningfully.

When I ask daughters why they don't know their fathers better or why they don't talk more with him about personal things, most say: "Because he doesn't want to talk about personal stuff." "He's just not a self-disclosing person." "He doesn't like to talk about his life." "He can't open up emotionally." Or "He doesn't want a deeper relationship with me." If you've ever felt this way, let me ask you this: Do you treat your father exactly like you treat your mother when it comes to the effort you put into getting to know them and allowing them to know you? For example, when's the last time you asked your father anything personal about his life—past or present? How often have you gone to him to share something personal that is going on in your life? Let the following quiz help you to assess how much effort you've put into getting to know your father and how willing you've been to allow him to know you.

If you score above 40, you're doing a terrific job treating your father in ways that make it easier for you to get to know each other. But if you score below 15, you're making it extremely difficult—if not almost impossible. If you score somewhere between 15 and 40, try doing the things on this checklist more often, and follow the advice in the rest of this chapter.

How Much Effort Have You Made?

In addressing the following issues, use 0 to mean "never," 1 to mean "rarely," 2 to mean "half the time," and 3 to mean "almost always."

Have you ever

____ told your dad as much as you tell your mom about what's going on in your life?

____ invited your dad to do things alone with you?

____ complimented your dad on what you appreciate about him?

____ let your dad know how much you value his opinion?

____ asked your dad what's going on in his life aside from his work?

____ shopped or done errands with your dad?

____ told your dad your deepest feelings?

____ asked for your dad's advice on personal matters?

____ written, phoned, or sent e-mails just to your dad?

____ asked your dad to tell you about his past?

____ let your dad know what you would like to have more of in your relationship?

____ responded enthusiastically when your dad asks you questions about your life?

____ bought your dad gifts that show how well you've listened to what he's told you about himself?

____ contacted your dad for no other reason than to ask how he's doing?

____ contacted your dad to say that you love or appreciate him?

____ Your score (45 possible)

Eye Openers

- Many fathers spend more time with their sons than with their daughters.[1,10]
- Our society emphasizes mother-daughter relationships more than father-daughter relationships.[10–14]
- Most children's books, TV programs, and movies send the message that fathers and daughters are not supposed to know each other as well as mothers and daughters.[15–19]

Step 2: Spend More Time Alone with Dad

There's a joke about two people trying to get to know each other. After spending time together, with a disappointed look on her face, the first person says, "You know, I told you to be yourself around me—but if this is who you are, please be somebody else!" Kidding aside, as you and your father are getting to know each other better, you won't necessarily like everything you discover. But that's part of being emotionally intimate—seeing each other's flaws, accepting the imperfections in each other. Think about it: Don't you usually feel closer to a person when the two of you have shared your imperfections with each other?

Regardless of your age, the most important thing you can do to create more emotional intimacy is to spend more time alone with your dad and to use this time alone to ask him more meaningful questions. This sounds simple enough. But if you're like many daughters, you're not very comfortable spending time alone with your dad "just talking." When you do spend time alone with him, you're usually doing something that makes it difficult to have a private conversation about anything personal or serious. Think about it. The last time you had a meaningful or intimate conversation with a friend, what were the two of you doing while you were talking? What kind of setting were you in? Was anyone else nearby to eavesdrop on your conversation? Now think about your father. When was the last time you and he were in a situation such as the one you just described? How often do you try to talk to him when no other family member is around— nobody who can interrupt, take over, judge, or steer the conversation in a different direction?

Daughters repeatedly tell me how meaningful it is to finally start talking to their fathers without anyone else around. This daughter's comments represent what many others have said to me: "Before I started to ask my father the questions you gave us, he said half jokingly, 'I'll tell you one thing. The only way I'll answer is if *you know who* isn't around.' Of course, he was talking about my mother, and he said it while all three of us were standing in the kitchen. We all laughed, even my mom. But his simple comment drove home to me the importance of establishing equal but separate relationships with my parents. He wanted to tell his stories to his daughter without my mom piping in with 'Wait, wait, you've got that all wrong. Oh, you forgot to tell her . . .' From now on I'm making a promise to myself not to treat him like a second-rate parent. When I have something to tell him, I'll find time alone with him, or I'll call him at work so that we can have our privacy."

If spending time alone with your father makes you uncomfortable, try easing into it by inviting him to do these sorts of things alone with you:

- Show you how to do something that he enjoys or does well—something as simple as trimming plants, grilling steaks his special way, or playing a card game.

- Go to a religious service alone with you.

- Tag along with him for a few hours while he does errands.

- Go to a movie together—share a box of popcorn.

- Take you back to the neighborhood where he grew up and walk around together.

- Visit the cemetery where a relative or close friend of his is buried.

- Get a camera or camcorder and go off for a few hours to take pictures of places that mean a lot to you or him.

Step 3: Get Personal—Ask Meaningful Questions

If you feel nervous about asking your dad personal questions, that's okay. *Do it anyway.* Many daughters have told me that their fathers don't want to be asked about anything personal. Almost all are shocked to discover that their fathers welcome the chance to share their stories, to express their feelings, and to answer their daughters' serious and emotional questions—*as long as nobody else is around.* If your dad hasn't seemed very interested in talking about personal things or about himself, maybe it's because you haven't taken enough time *alone* with him to ask those meaningful, personal questions. Or maybe you only ask in a joking, teasing way. In any case, don't let your nervousness or your negative assumptions about how he's going to react stop you from trying to get to know him at a deeper level. Just do it!

Here are two ideas to help you get started. First, invite your father to go somewhere alone with you. Take him out to lunch (your treat), or fix a picnic and go to a quiet spot, or take a long walk together. Whatever you choose, be sure there are no distractions that might interfere with your being able to talk privately. Second, ask your dad to choose 10 pictures from different times of his life—especially his childhood and teenage years. Be sure to ask him to include a picture of his father. Do *not* ask your mother to choose the pictures. If your father says that he'll get your mother to do it, tell him it would mean a lot to you if he would choose the pictures on his own. Remember, your "lion" needs the chance to tell his own story—and that means having him choose the pictures that he finds the most meaningful. In fact, many daughters learn a lot about their fathers just from which pictures they choose. As you're looking at the pictures together (with nobody else around), ask him what was going on in his life at the time. If he seems tense, or if he gives you really short answers, help him along by saying such things as: "Tell me more about that. What was that like? Why was that? How did that make you feel? What happened next? How did that come about? What was going on before then? How do you feel about that now?" By the way, did you know that many fathers say their own fathers never said "I love you" to them?[20–22] This is something you might want to ask your own father about. Anyway, remember that nobody should be around while you and your dad are talking, and you should set aside plenty of time.

How safe and relaxed your father feels opening up to you has a lot to do with what kinds of questions you ask and how you word your questions. The questions in the following box can lift your conversation above the superficial, impersonal stuff. You can use my questions in several ways. You can read them before you talk to your dad so that you have a clear idea of what to ask and how to word it. You might even write a couple of them on a small piece of paper to take along when you go off alone with him to talk—especially if it's a touchy topic that you want to word "just right." Or you can give your father a list of questions ahead of time and ask him to choose a few he'd most like to talk about. You might feel a little silly doing this. And your dad might tease you or act like it's a dumb idea. Just trust me on this: When daughters give the questions to their fathers ahead of time in writing, the men usually give more meaningful, more personal answers because they have had time to think about their feelings and experiences. Because most fathers aren't used to their daughters asking them personal or emotional questions, your dad might say something like: "But you already know me, so what's there to talk about?" or "I can't remember—just ask your mother." In return, you can say: "Dad, I don't want to hear about your life from someone else. I want you to tell me" or "Even if you think I know you, I want to know you better."

Let me tell you about Alice's success in getting her dad to open up through a silly "game" I recommended to her. Alice's father was in his sixties and living across the country, which meant that they rarely got to see each other. As I suggested, she asked her dad if he'd be willing to phone her on the last Sunday of every month when he could get at least 30 minutes completely alone to talk with her. At the beginning of each month, they each mailed the other 10 questions that they would most like to discuss about the other's life. Then, on the designated Sunday, each of them answered whichever three questions they most wanted to address. At first, Alice's dad said that the idea sounded goofy. But he was willing to give it a try. As it turned out, they usually ended up discussing all the questions. And after a few months, when Alice suggested that they just ask each other the questions instead of writing them down ahead of time, her dad objected: "No, honey. To tell you the truth, I like you writing the questions down and sending them to me so that I have time to think about them carefully." What had started out as a silly game that her father felt uncomfortable with had became a way of creating emotional intimacy.

Getting Your Lion to Talk: Questions for Your Father

His Childhood and Family

1. Who is (or was) your favorite relative? Why?
2. What do you like and dislike about each of your parents?
3. How are you like and unlike each of your parents?
4. What are three of your favorite childhood memories?
5. How did each of your parents show they loved you?
6. What were your father's hopes for you?
7. What did you get too little of from your father? What did you get too much of?
8. What kind of relationship did you have with your father? With your mother?
9. What have you had to forgive your father for? And your mother?
10. How are you and your siblings alike and different? Why do you think this is?
11. What is something you wish—or would have wished—for your father? Your mother?
12. What were some of your favorite childhood toys or games?
13. Who were your best friends and your enemies as a child and teenager?
14. Other than a relative, who was especially kind to you as a child and a teenager?
15. What was your best and your worst birthday while you were growing up?

His Values

16. What book, film, and piece of music has affected you the most? Why?
17. What's your favorite time of day? Why?
18. If you had a motto, what would it be?
19. If you could afford it, what would you buy or do?
20. What do you wish you had more of? Why?
21. What are your three most important possessions?

(*Continued*)

22. What are your opinions on welfare, the death penalty, legal drinking age, and interracial marriage?
23. How do you define yourself politically?
24. What three people do you admire? Why?
25. If you could change two laws, what would they be?
26 What would bring you the greatest joy during the next few years?

His Friends

27. What are four traits you look for in a friend?
28. Who have you known longest, and why has your friendship lasted so long?
29. Which friend do you miss most? Why?
30. What is the best advice a friend ever gave you?
31. Which friend knows you the best, frustrates you most, and is most unlike you?
32. What have friends done that hurt you the most, and how did you deal with that?
33. What does it take for you to forgive a friend?
34. What things do you have the hardest time forgiving?
35. How do you show love and anger to your friends?
36. What do your friends like the most and the least about you?
37. What would you like to say to one of your friends if you wouldn't have to pay a price for it?
38. What do you feel most ashamed of doing to a friend?
39. What are some of the best things your friends have ever done for you?
40. How have your friendships changed since you were my age?
41. What are some of your saddest experiences with friends?

His Spiritual Beliefs

42. How have your religious beliefs changed over time?
43. What was your most spiritual experience?
44. What spiritual questions do you ask yourself most often?
45. How would you like to spend the last 3 years of your life? The last 3 hours of your life?

46. Other than relatives, who would you like to see during the last years of your life?
47. What do you hope people will remember most about you?
48. How would you want your funeral arranged?
49. What are your greatest worries about aging or dying?
50. How has another person's death affected your own religious views or feelings about dying?
51. How has your parents' aging or dying affected you?
52. If you could have any two spiritual questions answered, what would they be?
53. What were your spiritual beliefs when you were my age?

His Feelings About Himself

54. How successful do you consider yourself? Why?
55. What are your best and worst traits?
56. How do you think you developed those traits?
57. What are some of the best compliments you've ever gotten?
58. As a child and teenager, what were some of your most peaceful moments? Jealous? Angriest? Tragic? Desperate? Happiest? Proudest? Most embarrassing? Most frightening?
59. What three things do you wish you had done differently in regard to your work?
60. What are three of the best and three of the worst decisions you've ever made?
61. What are four of the most unselfish things you've ever done?
62. What three lessons did you learn the hard way?
63. What do you wish you could do just by just snapping your fingers?
64. What dream have you had more than once? What do you think it means?
65. What do you think a lot about nowadays? As a teenager? When you were my age?
66. Other than family, what people have had the greatest influence on you?

(*Continued*)

67. What four adjectives would you use to describe your personality?
68. What aspects of your personality do you wish you could change and why?

His Romantic Life

69. What were the best and worst dating experiences you had before your got married?
70. How do you feel about people living together or having sex before marriage?
71. How do you feel about gay and lesbian relationships?
72. What romantic relationships had the greatest impact on you, and how?
73. What do you wish had been different about your romantic relationships?
74. How liberal or conservative do you consider yourself to be on sexual issues?
75. How have your ideas about love, sex, and marriage changed over time?
76. What do you wish you had known about sexual and romantic relationships as a young man?
77. What have your strengths and weaknesses been as a romantic partner or husband?
78. What were the most heart-breaking experiences you had in your romantic life?

Step 4: Overcome Your Fear of Discussing "It"

I've never known a daughter who didn't have an "it"—that one topic that she or her father are afraid to discuss. For some, "it" is alcoholism, depression, adultery, cancer, anorexia, divorce, death, dad's tour of duty in Viet Nam, or his feelings about her boyfriend, sex, or religion. Whatever your "it" is, you or your father probably do wish that you could talk about it. The problem is that you're uncomfortable bringing "it" up. You don't know how to start. You're also afraid. Afraid of what? Until you figure that out, you can't get "it" out into the open. "It" will remain packed away in the secret closet where your other family skeletons are hidden from view. Out of sight, yes, but not out of mind. Many daughters tell me that they're afraid to bring "it" up because someone else in the family has told them not to: "Don't bring that up with you father. You'll only upset him." "Don't ask him about that because he doesn't want to discuss it with you." Although these people mean well, please ignore their advice. Until you have tried at least once to raise the topic with your father—and *only when the two of you are completely alone*—don't be frightened off by what others have told you about how your father is going to react. Please give the man a chance to speak for himself. He is not a child who needs someone else in your family to speak for him or to predict how he is going to behave.

Even though I don't know your father, I can tell you that almost every daughter I have given this advice to has been glad that she followed it. Despite their negative assumption that men don't want to talk about personal or emotional things, their fathers were relieved to finally get a chance to get "it" out in the open. Yes, your father may get sad or be at a loss for words for a few minutes. He may even cry. If you see how sad, how fragile, or how vulnerable he is, you may be tempted to change the topic, stop the conversation, or do something to lighten things up. You might feel like leaving the room. You might look away from him as if you're embarrassed. Please don't do these things. Sit still. Reach out and touch his shoulder or his hand. Don't withdraw from him when he's opening up to you. Allow him to be emotional and fragile—not the heroic, all-knowing, invincible "daddy" from your childhood.

Maybe these two daughters' experiences will give you the courage to talk to your dad about "it."

Nadia's Story

I was extremely nervous to talk to my dad about his having had prostate cancer last year. I presumed that he would feel uncomfortable talking about something so personal. Surprisingly, he didn't skip a beat. Letting him know how frightened I had been was such a relief, but hearing his side of the story was much more significant. His openness in talking about such a difficult topic gives me confidence to go to him with serious, complicated problems from now on. His ability to put me at ease was so incredible and so surprising.

Trudy's Story

I always knew that my parents had a baby who had died before I was born. I never thought I should ask about it. But finally I did. I had never heard my dad talk like he did that night with me. I could see the hurt in his eyes and hear the shakiness in his voice—even after so many years. Suddenly I understood why my dad had always been such a germ freak. It had stemmed from the baby's death, because nobody ever figured out why she had died. Dad said the one question he would like to ask God is why He took away his baby. As Dad and I were talking, I realized that I have believed those negative stereotypes about fathers that you talked to me about. I was so wrong to assume that he wouldn't want to talk about his weaknesses or the times in life when he was hurt.

The next exercise can help you to figure out what you're afraid might happen if you and your dad discuss "it." For example, you may be afraid that he will cry or that someone else in the family will be upset by what you and he talk about. Or you may be afraid that there will be these long, awkward silences where neither of you will know what to say next. After you imagine the worst that might happen, imagine the best. For example, you two might feel more relaxed around each other or you might forgive each other for things that have been limiting your relationship.

Why I'm Afraid to Discuss "It"

Three things I'd like to discuss with dad if I knew the outcome would be good:

1. _____

2. _____

3. _____

The worst things I can imagine happening if we talked are:

1. _____
2. _____
3. _____

The best things I can imagine happening if we talked are:

1. _____
2. _____
3. _____

Step 5: Discuss Your Relationship

One topic that many daughters are afraid to discuss with their father is their father-daughter relationship. What's good about it—and what isn't? What does each of you wish was different? How could you make those things happen? What do you each want more of—and what do you want less of? Before you try to discuss your relationship, ask him more general questions about what it has been like being a father. Gradually move on to the more personal questions about your relationship. Use the following questions to get the conversation going and move to a more intimate level.

Questions About Fatherhood and About Our Relationship

About Being a Father

1. What has been the most fun about being a father?
2. How has being a father changed you?
3. As a young father, what worried you the most?
4. What do you wish you had known before you became a father?
5. How well do you think you fit our society's definition of a good father?
6. What are your greatest strengths and weaknesses as a father?

(*Continued*)

7. How did your relationship with your dad influence the kind of parent you have been?
8. What advice would you give, on the basis of your experiences, to younger fathers?
9. How has being a father to a son been different from being a father to a daughter?
10. How have your ideas and your behavior as a father changed over the years?

About Our Relationship

1. What was the best gift and compliment I ever gave you?
2. What was hardest about being my father when I was an infant? A teenager? Now?
3. How did our relationship change as I was growing up?
4. What do you wish we had more of in our relationship now?
5. What do you wish you and I had done differently in our relationship?
6. What do you wish had been different about our relationship as I was growing up? Now?
7. What do you wish I had understood better about you as I was growing up? Now?
8. What are some of the saddest and happiest experiences you've had with me?
9. What questions do you wish I had asked you about our relationship?
10. What questions are you glad I didn't ask you? (You don't have to answer them.)

Before you talk with your father about anything you want to change about your relationship, be sure that you know exactly what it is you want. In Chapter 3 you learned how to ask your father for what you want. Now you have to figure out what you want to ask for. The exercises in the box can help you do that. You also might ask your father to write down his answers to the exercises before the two of you actually talk. Even if the two of you disagree on how to go about getting more of what you want from your relationship, discussing these exercises together probably will show that you both want a lot of the same things.

The Perfect Day Together

What is the most perfect day you can imagine the two of you having together? Don't think about the obstacles. Just let your imagination run free.

- Where would the two of you be?
- What would you do for the entire day?
- What would each of you do to make the other feel loved?
- What would each of you be feeling as the day started out?
- What would each of you be feeling when the day ended?
- How would your family feel and react to your having such a wonderful day together?
- What would each of you say that you've never said before?
- What would be the highlight of the day?
- What would each of you do or bring as a nice surprise for one another?
- What are the last words each of you would say at the end of the day?

Wish Lists: Yours and His

What three things do each of you enjoy most about your relationship?

Me

1. _____
2. _____
3. _____

Dad

1. _____
2. _____
3. _____

(*Continued*)

What three things would each of you like changed or improved?

Me

1. _____
2. _____
3. _____

Dad

1. _____
2. _____
3. _____

What three things could each of you do differently to strengthen your relationship?

Me

1. _____
2. _____
3. _____

Dad

1. _____
2. _____
3. _____

Our Best and Worst Times Together

What are three situations where your father did something that hurt your relationship?

1. _____
2. _____
3. _____

What do you wish he had done in each situation?

1. _____
2. _____

3. _____

What would he have to do *now* to make you feel better about those past events? If it's something he would have to say, write out exactly what you'd want him to say.
1. _____
2. _____
3. _____

If you have not talked with your father about these situations, why haven't you (your fears)?
1. _____
2. _____
3. _____

What are three situations where your father did something that made you feel closer to him?
1. _____
2. _____
3. _____

Now repeat this exercise. Only this time look at those situations where *you* are the one who did something that hurt or helped your relationship.

Step 6: End the Secrecy and Deception

So far we've focused on how you can get to know your father better. But emotional intimacy means that you also have to allow him to get to know you better. How often do you tell your father about those parts of your life which matter most to you—your romantic partner, troubles with your close friends or coworkers, your spiritual views, or anything personal? I can't tell you how much to share with your parents about your life. Some daughters share almost everything. And others share almost nothing. This is not what concerns me. What concerns me is *equality*—that you give your father the same opportunities you give your mother to get to know you and that whatever you choose to share about your life, you share equally with both parents.

Do I hear you thinking: "Is she saying that I ought to tell my father the most intimate details of my life? Can't I have any privacy? Aren't there certain things daughters and fathers shouldn't let each other know?" Let me reassure you that privacy is a good thing. And you're right; you and your father shouldn't tell each other everything. All of us need a certain amount of privacy. For example, neither you nor your dad wants anyone opening your mail, eavesdropping on your phone conversations, rummaging through your belongings, or walking into your bedroom without knocking.

On the other hand, privacy shouldn't mean deceiving or lying to another person. For example, it's one thing if you don't tell your father the reasons why you got fired. You may feel that's a very private matter. But it's another thing if you lie to him outright or lead him to believe that you haven't been fired. That's deception. You can maintain your privacy without being dishonest by saying such things to your father as: "I don't feel comfortable telling you about that part of my life" or "That part of my life is something I don't talk to anyone about, Dad." But if you lie when he specifically asks you about something, or you go to great lengths to hide information, or you pretend to believe things that you don't believe in, then you're being deceptive and dishonest—not private. Privacy doesn't detract from your emotional intimacy with your father. Deception and dishonesty do.

Pretending can be one of the most damaging kinds of deception because you end up living the lies rather than just telling them. Even though you don't have to disclose everything about yourself to someone you love, the more emotionally intimate a relationship is, the more you generally want the other person to know who you are. And you don't have the stress or run the risk of damaging your relationship when you eventually "get found out" for being who you are. When you hide too much about yourself from you father, he doesn't get a chance to know you in the truest or the deepest sense. And if you often put on an act or fake it around your father, you end up feeling like a phony—an imposter. So even if your "act" succeeds in making your dad happy (or keeping him from getting unhappy), you haven't really succeeded at all because you know he's not reacting to you. He's reacting to the phony—the imposter. That's not much of a victory, is it?

Keeping secrets from your father also can be a way of deceiving him. Again, privacy doesn't damage relationships, but secrecy usually does. Even when the hidden information isn't really very important, the person being excluded is being treated like an outsider—like someone we don't trust. Secrets say more about how you feel about the people you tell or don't tell them to than about the importance of the information itself. Think about it: How do you feel when your close friend shares a secret with someone else but not with you? How do you feel when you're the last one to be let in on the secret? What if your friend has told her secret to almost everyone else except you? Even if the secret information was trivial, how does being left out make you feel about your friendship?

As for your father, how would you feel if he shared secrets with one of your siblings but not with you? What impact could it have on your relationship if you found out that your dad had been hiding many of the most important things about himself from you? When it comes to secrets, do you treat him like an insider or like an outsider? Is he usually the last one you share your secrets with? Do you and your mother hide information from him, treating him as if he were a child or a heartless judge? What might your dad be feeling when he senses that he isn't being let in on your secrets when others are? How much of the really "big" stuff are you hiding from him—things like being raped, having an eating disorder, being clinically depressed, having a drinking problem, being on the verge of a divorce, losing your job, or having major financial problems.

If lying, deceiving, keeping secrets, or pretending to be someone they're not can be so damaging, why do many daughters behave this way around their fathers? Most tell me that it's because they don't want to hurt, anger, or disappoint him: "I don't want dad to think less of me" "I don't want to upset him," "He would be ashamed of me if he knew the real me." "He'd be furious if he found out what I really believe." Others truly believe that their fathers will love them less if they stop pretending or stop deceiving them:

"He could never love me the way he does now if he really knew me" or "I honestly believe that he would cut me out of his will and never see me again if he knew who I really was."

If you've ever felt this way, ask yourself these questions: Is it possible that I could be wrong about my dad—possible that he is capable of loving me just as much even if he does know "the truth" about me? Is there any chance that if I pretended less and deceived him less, we might actually develop a more relaxed, more honest relationship? Am I absolutely certain that my father is incapable of having a loving relationship with me just because I tell him things about me that disappoint or anger him?

As you're doing the activity in this next box, ask yourself if anyone in your family might be encouraging you to deceive or to keep secrets from your father. Maybe someone is sending you messages such as these: "Dad won't understand, so don't tell him." "Let's just keep this between us because it would upset your dad." "Your dad can't handle it, so let's not let him know." These people may mean well, but try to free yourself from their influence. Give your father the chance to know you before assuming the worst about how he might react.

How Truthful Are You with Each Other?

How truthful are you with your father about these aspects of your life? In addressing these issues, use 0 to mean "not at all," 1 to mean "sometimes," 2 to mean "half the time," and 3 to mean "almost always."

____ Money

____ Drinking

____ Mental problems

____ Sex

____ Smoking

____ Political beliefs

____ Health issues

___ Romantic relationships

___ Job or school

___ Religion

When you or your dad aren't being honest, what do you usually do to hide the truth?

Dad Me

___ ___ Change the topic

___ ___ Withhold information

___ ___ Tell part of the truth

___ ___ Conceal the evidence so as not to get caught

___ ___ Mislead, distort, or misrepresent

___ ___ Lie outright

Step 7: Apologize and Forgive

It's been said that "Nature didn't make us perfect, so it did the next best thing by making us blind to our own flaws." As you get to know each other better, you and your father may realize that both of you have some apologizing and some forgiving to do. To forgive—what does that mean? For me, forgiving doesn't mean forgetting or pretending that certain things never happened. Forgiving means being willing to stop punishing the other person—to stop withholding love, refusing to talk to them, asking them to apologize over and over again, or reminding them repeatedly about what they did. Forgiving means confronting some tough questions: How willing are you to let the other person off the hook for his or her mistakes? How long is "long enough" to stay angry or to keep punishing him or her—another year, another 10 years, or a lifetime? Are you unwilling to forgive because clinging to your anger serves some purpose for you? Maybe staying angry allows you to blame your father for things that go wrong in your life rather than having to face your own shortcomings.

I can't answer these questions for you. But I can tell you this: When people apologize, the forgiveness that follows strengthens the relationship.[23, 24] Here's what one daughter whose father had almost torn their family apart because of his alcoholism wrote about forgiveness:

> *When I asked my father what the best gift I ever gave him was, he told me it was a paper I had written in high school on forgiveness. I had almost forgotten about it; but to him it was the most special thing I have ever done for him. I truly believe that everyone has the right to be forgiven if they are truly remorseful—and he was. Good people make bad decisions sometimes, and my relationship with my father has just grown stronger over time because we both love each other despite mistakes we have both made.*

If you feel that your relationship would benefit if your father apologized to you for something he has done, you need to take these steps: First, be absolutely certain that he knows what it is he did that is still upsetting you. It's possible that your father honestly does not know that you're upset with him. Or he might assume that you've gotten over it by now. Second, tell him how his behavior made you feel—unloved, unappreciated, frightened, or jealous. Third, let him know how much his apology would mean to you. Fourth, tell him exactly what he would have to say or do for you to forgive him. These suggestions may sound ridiculous to you, but I've known many a daughter who readily admitted to me that her father had no idea that she was still upset with him—or admitted that he knew she was upset but didn't know exactly what he did that upset her—or admitted that he had tried to apologize but somehow didn't "do it right."

Of course, apologies need to go the other way sometimes. *You* may be the one who owes an apology to your father. So what's stopping you? Many daughters tell me that they know they owe their dad an apology. And they know that apologizing would strengthen the relationship. Many say that they haven't apologized because they believe that once they admit they were wrong, their fathers will "hold it over my head forever." Others are afraid that their fathers won't forgive them anyway, so why go through the humiliation or pain of apologizing when there's no reward afterwards? But look at it this way: When your father apologizes to you, *he has to take these same risks.* He has no guarantee that you won't hold it over his head or keep bringing up his mistake even though he has humbled himself by apologizing to you. Then, too, why refuse to apologize to him because you assume the worst about how he is going to react? You wouldn't like it if he did this to you, would you?

Some daughters tell me that they did apologize but that "it didn't make any difference to my dad." When I get them to tell me about the way they apologized, I realize that they didn't go about it in a way that showed remorse, compassion, or a genuine desire to change. So here are six essential ingredients for the "ideal" apology [23-25]

1. *Don't shift the blame:* "Well, I'm sorry, dad, but if you hadn't done such and such, then I wouldn't have done such and such." *Do accept the responsibility for what you did:* "I'm sorry, dad. I know *I* shouldn't have. . . ."

2. Don't apologize for hurting the person's feelings: "I'm sorry if your feelings are hurt, dad." Do apologize for what you did: "I'm sorry that I. . . ."

3. *Don't trivialize the damage you did:* "It was really no big deal, dad, so I don't know why you're so upset." *Do show that you understand how he feels:* "I realize how much I hurt you, dad, when I did that."

4. *Don't take the focus away from his feelings by talking about how awful you feel about what you did:* "I'm such an awful human being for doing what I did. I know you'll never forgive me. I haven't been able to eat for 3 days because of this." *Do keep the focus on his feelings.*

5. *Don't criticize him as you're apologizing:* "I'm truly sorry I behaved that way, dad; but you've done the same thing to me. Why just last week. . . ."

6. *Don't rely only on a verbal apology.* Do something to try to make up for your mistake.

Will It Be Worth It?

If you follow through on the suggestions in this chapter, will it be worth it? How well have my suggestions worked for other daughters? Let me

Forgiving and Apologizing

What three things do you wish your father would apologize for? How long ago did they happen?

1. _____
2. _____
3. _____

What three things do you owe your father an apology for? How long ago did they happen?

1. _____
2. _____
3. _____

What are three reasons why your father hasn't apologized yet?

1. _____
2. _____
3. _____

What are three reasons why you haven't apologized to him yet?

1. _____
2. _____
3. _____

Other than apologizing, what else would your father have to do for you to forgive him?

_____

Other than apologizing, what would you have to do for him to forgive you?

_____

Eye Openers

- Some daughters cannot apologize or forgive until their father is very ill or dying.[26–29]
- Even as very young children, some people are much better than others at forgiving and empathizing.[26,27]
- Males are just as forgiving, as compassionate, and as empathic as females.[27–29]

answer by sharing what daughters have said about spending time alone with their fathers to ask them more meaningful, personal questions.

Father's Childhood

Sue: "I had never seen pictures of him as a child—so small and vulnerable. When I got him talking about his dad, I saw him fight not to show me his pain. I actually reached over to him and said it was okay to talk to me about it. It was such a weird moment—me reaching out to my dad for the first time."

Jody: "As I got him to talk about his childhood, I realized that my dad was a victim of vicious cycles in his own family. It's hard now to be angry with him over things he never learned how to do."

Sarah: "The thing that glaringly stood out for me was how negative an impact my father's childhood had on him. My dad still seems to be acting in ways to prove to his dead father that he can be successful."

Father's Young Adult Life

Joanne: "It made me so sad to hear him say that even when he was my age, he had no dreams. I got a glimpse into the darkness and emptiness inside him."

Lorraine: "I'd always thought of him as a prude. But after listening to his stories about the wild things he did when he was younger, I actually see the carefree man in there."

Lou: "His stories were so meaningful because I am struggling with the same questions as he did when he was my age. I also saw him as a young man remembering what it was like to fall in love. There was such tenderness in his voice."

Jen: "As I listened to him, I was finally able to imagine him as a 21-year-old with no responsibility or medical initials after his name—young and jovial, playing the drums, eyeing the girls. He used to dream of being a free spirit, a famous athlete, and a wealthy tycoon. Who knew?"

His Life Beyond the Family

Lynne: "As I listened to him, I began to see my father as a person who struggles through life as a man and a husband—not just as my father. When we were discussing his dreams, the expressive look on his face and his tone of voice made me see him as a man with a lonely heart. It meant so much to have him open up to me just for that short time."

Trish: "For the first time ever we talked about religion. I saw what a deep person he is. I was thoroughly intrigued by what he was telling me. Yesterday I wrote and told him how much our talk meant to me."

Paula: "I was surprised to learn that he still sees his life as a developing process—even at his age. I'd never thought he was introspective, and now I find out he is. I don't know why I haven't asked him these questions before. I feel so much closer to him now."

Father's Openness

Sally: "When I first started asking him personal questions about himself, he was sitting with his legs and arms tightly crossed. But he literally opened up physically and emotionally the more we talked. By the end of our hours together, his feet were propped up, his arms were on the arm rests, and he was open and relaxed."

Arlene: "When I first told my dad I wanted to spend a few hours alone with him to ask him questions about his life, he laughed at me. But he did it. It ended up being the first time we've ever talked to each other about his life for more than 10 minutes."

Marty: "As we talked, I realized that he and I have been wanting the same thing from our relationship all these years, but that we never talked enough to figure that out."

Anna: "It was very moving when my dad said the nicest gift I ever gave him was deciding finally that I want to get to know him. At the end of our time together, he gave a big sigh and said, 'I was really nervous about answering some of your questions. I mean, we have never really talked alone like this before now.'"

No matter how old you and your father are now, getting to know each other on a more personal, more emotionally intimate level will deepen your bond. By drawing your father out and by allowing him in, you are embracing your relationship more lovingly and more fully.

Chapter 5

Your Mother's Power
Don't Build a Road to Dad Through Mom

- Do you usually go to your mother when you're upset with your dad?

- Did you ever feel that your mom did more than her fair share in raising you?

- Has your mother ever seemed a little jealous of your relationship with your father?

- Did you ever get the feeling that your mother thought she was a better parent than your father?

- Are you uncomfortable thinking about your mother's influence on your father-daughter relationship?

If so, you can strengthen your father-daughter relationship by considering the impact your mother has had and by changing the way you relate to your father through your mother. This chapter will show you how your mother has influenced the kind of relationship you have with your father—and how you can create a more personal, more relaxed relationship with him by relating to her and to him differently. Before going any further, I want to be sure that you understand my intent. My intent is not to blame mothers for whatever isn't right in father-daughter relationships. Blaming someone implies that the person intentionally set out to do harm. Blaming also assumes that the person is aware of what he or she is doing and aware of the negative impact he or she might be having. Because no parent is perfect, there probably are certain things your mother could have done differently to strengthen your relationship with your father even more. But rather than blaming her, you can strengthen your relationship with you father by recognizing any negative influence your mother may have had and by using this awareness to change the ways you interact with each of your parents.

As we begin to consider the impact that our mothers have had on our father-daughter relationships, let's keep these facts from earlier chapters in mind:

- Women who choose not to have children are just as happy and well adapted as mothers.[1]

- Daughters and mothers are usually closer and know one another better than daughters and fathers.[2–4]

- Well-educated white mothers tend to be more jealous and insecure about "sharing" the children with their fathers than less well educated or nonwhite mothers.[5,6]

Your Mother's Upbringing and Mental Health

Because mothers have so much power over the kinds of relationships children develop with their fathers, researchers have spent a good deal of time figuring out which mothers are the most supportive. As you think about your own mother, you'll be able to see why she has or has not been able to support your having just as close a relationship with your father as you have with her. Generally speaking, your mother will allow and encourage you and your dad to have the closest possible relationship if she:

- Was raised by loving, happily married parents[7,8]

- Had a full-time job while you were growing up[9,10]

- Is African-American or from a culture where mothers feel comfortable and appreciate other adults helping to raise the kids[5,11]

- Is relatively content with her life and free from depression[12]

How many of these characteristics applied to your mother *during your childhood?* The more of these characteristics she had, the closer you and your father probably are in large part because your mother allowed and encouraged him to be as involved with you as she was. When your mother had loving, happily married parents and when she worked full time outside the home after you kids were born, good things probably happened for you and your dad. Your mom was more likely to stand back and allow your dad to be an equal parent. From the time you were born, she actively and enthusiastically shared the parenting—allowing your father equal power and an equal voice. Instead of criticizing, supervising, or correcting the way he did things with you kids, she complimented and appreciated him. Even though they related to you kids in different ways, she rarely criticized or ridiculed his way of parenting. On the other hand, if your mother stayed home during most of your childhood, or if she did not have loving relationships with her own parents, there is a greater chance that she was jealous, competitive, threatened, or insecure when your father tried to be as involved with you as she was. She may have acted as if she was the most important parent—the expert on raising children. And she may have turned to you kids for nurturing, comfort, self-esteem, advice, help, and emotional intimacy. This kind of "closeness" with your mom generally creates more distance between you and your dad—sometimes creating a pattern where you side with her against him. Growing up, you may have tended to see your mother as more self-sacrificing, vulnerable, and powerless than your father. If so, you probably have a more distant or strained relationship with your father than you would have had otherwise. The following quiz can help you to remember back to your mother's well-being during most of your childhood.

The higher her score, the more likely it is that your mother enthusiastically supported your having just as close a relationship with your dad as you had with her. Her high score means that she felt secure, relaxed, and satisfied enough to stand back and let your father and you become closely bonded. The lower her score, the more likely she is to have felt that you should be much closer to her than to your father—and to have felt jealous, threatened, or insecure unless she—not your father—was always "number one" in your eyes.

How Is Mom Doing?

For most of your childhood, how would you describe your mother? In addressing the following issues, use 0 to mean "never," 1 to mean "sometimes," 2 to mean "quite a bit," and 3 to mean "often/almost always."

_____ Upbeat and generally content

_____ Self-reliant and confident

_____ Pleased with parts of her life aside from being a mother

_____ Physically healthy and energetic

_____ Interested in her work outside the home

_____ In love and happy with her husband

_____ Free from depression

_____ Happy with her relationship with her parents

_____ Satisfied with her life overall

_____ Emotionally sturdy and stable

_____ Score (30 possible)

Your Mother's Beliefs

As you may remember from Chapter One, what your parents believed about father-daughter relationships while you were growing up has a powerful impact on the kind of relationship you and your dad have had. More important still: Your mother's beliefs and feelings generally have as much or more power than your father's in shaping your father-daughter relationship.[13,14] Use the following quiz to consider the attitudes of mothers who do the most to strengthen father-daughter relationships.

The lower your mom's score, the more likely it is that she enthusiastically supported and encouraged your relationship with your dad. Because she believed that men could be excellent parents, she behaved in ways that helped you see the best in your dad and that made him feel welcomed and confident as a parent. For example, if your mother believed that men had just as much "instinct" or "intuition" as women have for raising children, then she probably treated your father and you as if he was just as nurturing and just as wise a parent as she was. And that's good for your father-daughter relationship. On the other hand, if your mom believed that women were

Mom's Beliefs: Helping or Hurting?

Which of these beliefs did your mother hold while you were growing up? In addressing the following statements, use 0 to mean "no," 1 to mean "maybe," and 2 to mean "definitely."

____ Unlike men, women have a natural instinct or intuition for raising children.

____ Mothers and daughters ought to have a closer, move involved relationship than fathers and daughters.

____ Mothers sacrifice more than fathers do for their kids.

____ Mothers are more stressed than fathers are trying to balance work and family.

____ Employed mothers do much more housework and child care than their husbands.

____ Daughters raised mainly by their mother are better off than those raised mainly by their father.

____ Mothers want to spend more time with their kids and less time at work, unlike fathers.

____ Children are better off when their mother stays home and their father earns the family's income.

____ Mothers enjoy being parents more than fathers do.

____ Mothers are more understanding and more nurturing than fathers.

____ Score (20 possible)

superior to men as parents, then she probably treated your father and you in ways that made it harder for you and him to become closely bonded. At this point in your life, you can strengthen your relationship by examining any negative beliefs about men as parents that you may have picked up from your mother as you were growing up.

The most important question to ask yourself is this: How comfortable was my mother with the possibility that my dad and I might become just as close as she and I were? The important word here is *close*. By close I do *not* mean *good, loving, or getting along well*. By close I mean sharing personal information, sharing what goes on in your day-to-day lives, and spending lots of time together just talking without anyone else in the family being around. Your mom probably wasn't jealous or threatened when you and your dad went off to "play" together—golf, ski, dive, or jog—because you probably weren't being emotionally intimate with him at those times. You and your dad weren't intruding onto your mom's "emotional territory." Sadly, though, there are mothers who feel uncomfortable or jealous with the idea that their daughter might share as much emotionally or personally with her father.[15-17]

If your mother felt (or feels) this way, you and your father may feel uncomfortable doing things together that might make your mom jealous or insecure. You may not spend much time with one another without including her. You may limit most of your conversations to impersonal topics—cars, money, sports, movies, school, or jobs—or you may only talk to your dad about personal things *after* you have already told your mom. Perhaps you resort to phoning or e-mailing your dad at work so that mom's feelings won't get hurt. If you ever sensed that your mom was jealous or uncomfortable in these ways, this doesn't mean that she was unloving or unkind. It just means that she felt jealous, threatened, or insecure when you seemed to be getting as close to your father as you were to her in these ways.

When I first mention this to daughters, most of them get defensive and protest that their mother isn't ever jealous. They claim that their mother has never done anything to detract from their father-daughter relationship. If this is how you feel, let me ask you this: How would your mother feel if you phoned and asked to speak to your father privately. Then you talk to him for an hour about something personal—trouble with your romantic partner, fear of being pregnant, or problems with your best friend. Along the same lines, how would your mother feel if you and your father decided to go off for a weekend by yourselves—or if he decided to visit you for a few days without bringing her along? If you and your father have never done this, why not? Haven't you and your mother spent time alone like this? So why not you and dad? Imagine what your mother's reactions would be. What would she say to you or to your father? How would she behave? If she didn't say anything to either of you, what do you think would be going on inside her head?

Here's what most young-adult daughters tell me: "If I asked to talk to dad on the phone, my mom would automatically think I wanted to talk about money. She'd be really hurt when she found out it was something personal." "She'd feel replaced, and her self worth would be diminished." "No way! My mother loves the position she holds—the one who has to know everything that's going on in the family." "She always has to be on the phone or in the room." "When dad and I are trying to talk, mom literally talks over him—almost like he didn't exist." "I couldn't do that because it would reinforce her insecurity about not having a career." "Mom would die if I ever talked to dad about my boyfriend instead of talking to her." "She would never say anything directly to me, but she'd let me know somehow that she was hurt."

As far as spending a few days alone with their fathers, most daughters in my course say: "I couldn't do it because mom has always wanted me to feel closer to her and need her most." "Now that she is off at work two days a week, my dad takes off from work early so we can spend time alone without her getting hurt. But that's as far as we can go." "When I tell her that dad and I are getting closer, I get the feeling that she thinks my relationship with him is just fine the way it is. I don't think she'd like our spending a weekend alone." "You've got to be kidding! My mom is already jealous just because I'm taking your fathers and daughters course. That's funny, because she doesn't mind that she and I often go out alone and talk without inviting dad." "She'd find some way to make dad feel guilty."

Your Mother's Feelings About Being Idealized

Aside from how your mother feels about your being as close to your dad as you are to her, how does she feel about admitting her shortcomings to you? Does she need you to see her as nearly perfect—the model of a "good" mother? Or is she comfortable with your seeing her mistakes and her human flaws? As we've discussed in earlier chapters, our society tends to idealize mothers—to cover up or to pretend that mothers can't be "bad" or have major flaws the way fathers or other adults who raise children do. [19,23] We tend to portray mothers as more unselfish, committed, understanding, loyal, faithful, honest, sweet hearted, sympathetic, approachable, insightful, trustworthy, and self-sacrificing than fathers.

Idealizing someone isn't the same as admiring, loving, or respecting them. Idealizing someone is usually an unhealthy situation in which you deny reality, create illusions, and lie to yourself and to others about your idol. You know you're idealizing someone when (1) you get extremely angry at anyone who points out your idol's flaws—whether that person is a therapist or a family member; (2) you cannot bear to think about the things you suspect (or know) this person has done wrong; (3) you're not able to tell anyone about your idol's mistakes or flaws because you want everyone to believe that this person is nearly perfect; (4) you create memories and stories about the past that are way out of line with what actually happened in order to maintain your illusions about this person; and (5) you generally blame other people for whatever mistakes your idol makes instead of holding that person accountable.

Ironically, we tend to idealize whichever parent has, in reality, done the most damage to the family and behaved the most selfishly and deceptively in order to create an image of himself or herself as good and blameless. But whichever parent you idealize, generally you can count on these things happening in your family: [18,19] Either you or one of your siblings is apt to become clinically depressed or chronically anxious. As adults, you may need a therapist's help to deal with problems caused by the secrecy, deception, denial, emotional manipulation, unspoken anger, alliances, and dishonest communication in your family. You can end up continually siding with your idealized parent against your other parent. At least one of you probably will become overly involved with your idealized parent. We psychologists refer to this unhealthy situation as being *enmeshed*. And being enmeshed with one of your parents damages your relationship with your other parent. Generally speaking, children are far more likely to become enmeshed with their mother than with their father. So it is the relationship with the father that suffers the most damage.

As children, we all idealize our parents. Idealizing them makes us feel safe. As we age, though, our parents need to make sure we outgrow these childish beliefs—that we see them realistically as imperfect human beings. This means that your father needs to let you know that he is not all-knowing, not a "Prince Charming," not a knight in shining armor. He needs to teach you that he is human—that he is sometimes weak, confused, frightened, foolish, fragile, vulnerable, or dependent. And your mother needs to do the same—to admit that she is not always a good mother and that you should not idealize her. Otherwise, we may continue to cling to the childish belief that mothers are the ideal model of the loving parent—a belief that can detract from our father-daughter relationships.

How good a job did your mother do teaching you that she is not what you imagined her to be when you were a little child? Has she made sure you know that she is sometimes just as selfish, unloving, deceitful, manipulative, untrustworthy, or petty as the rest of us? Has she made sure that you don't *automatically assume* that she is in the right and everyone else is in the wrong just because she is your mother? If your mother gives you this gift, you are likely to see your father in a more positive light because you are not idealizing your mother. By admitting her mistakes and imperfections rather than denying or covering them up, she allows you to perceive your father as loving and as lovable as she is. In contrast, if we idealize one parent, we often end up distancing ourselves from or failing to appreciate our other parent. And because our society tends to idealize motherhood more than fatherhood, we may have an especially hard time seeing our mothers realistically. [19,23]

As you mature, your mother should be willing to be increasingly honest with you about her flaws. If there have been serious problems in your family that have not been talked about openly, at some point your mother should encourage you to discuss them with her. For example, she might

say: "Do you have any questions about what's been going on in our family—or what went on in the past? Is there anything you'd like to know
about me that you've been too uncomfortable to ask?" If she is too uncomfortable or too embarrassed to share certain truths about herself with you,
that's all right, as long as she isn't creating illusions that might interfere in
your relationship with your father or with your well-being. For example,
let's assume that you have been blaming your father for your parents'
divorce when, in reality, your mother left him for another man. Once
you're an adult, she might say something like: "Look, I've done some
things that ended up hurting your relationship with your dad. I don't want
to continue denying or pretending anymore. I think it's time we talked
about the divorce, even though I may not be comfortable yet telling you
everything." In this way, your mother can protect her privacy without
allowing you to idealize her, without lying to you, and without asking you
to participate in a fantasy. By not allowing you to have illusions about her,
she is giving you and your father the chance to have a fuller, more loving
relationship because she is not presenting herself as the ideal or the perfect parent.

Generally speaking, your mother will not allow you to idealize or to
become enmeshed with her if she had a loving relationship with her own
parents while she was growing up and if she was relatively content with her
life while you were growing up. On the other hand, if she felt terribly guilty
about something she had done that she didn't want you to find out about,
or if she did not feel loved by her own parents, she is more likely to want
you to idealize her. [18,19]

Let me give you an example of what can happen when an adult daughter continues to idealize her mother. Jan had a very strained relationship
with her father even though her parents were still married. Although she
couldn't give me any examples of things her father had actually done to upset
or hurt her, she clearly blamed him for whatever was going wrong in her
family. In contrast, whenever Jan talked about her mother, she made the
woman sound like a saint—much like a young child describes a parent: "My
mom sacrifices so much for everyone. I've never met anyone as unselfish or
as loving as she is." She also claimed that her mother had never told a lie,
never deceived or manipulated anyone, and never done anything "really

wrong." It was clear that Jan was idealizing her mother, and as predicted, this had hurt her relationship with her father. As in most cases where an adult woman is idealizing her mother, Jan's mother was far from perfect. It eventually came out in our ongoing conversations that her mother had committed adultery, was often depressed, and had always found it difficult to relate sexually or emotionally to men because of her own troubled childhood. Jan denied that her mother could possibly have anything to do with her negative feelings about her father, with her sister's ongoing psychological problems, or with her own lack of self-confidence or self-reliance. Even as an adult, Jan was still clinging to the childlike belief that her mother was nearly perfect, even though this meant denying or excusing the "bad" things her mother had clearly done. And in the process Jan had distanced herself from her father.

Your Mother's Opinions of Your Father

Just as your father-daughter relationship benefits when your mother doesn't allow you to idealize her, it benefits when she considers your father to be just as good a parent as she is. As you were growing up, did your mother make you feel that your father was just as nurturing, approachable, understanding, knowledgeable, flexible, and sympathetic as she was? Did she let you know in no uncertain terms that she felt your father was every bit as good a parent as she was? Did she praise him in front of you, rather than criticize or make fun of him as a parent? Let's hope so, because a father usually has a closer relationship with his kids when the mother lets everyone in the family know how much she appreciates his ways of parenting—especially if his way of relating to the kids isn't exactly like hers. [13, 20]

In the following quiz you can see the many ways in which a mother strengthens the father-daughter relationship by relating to the father as her equal. The higher your mother's score, the more likely you are to have a close, open, comfortable relationship with your father. Her high score means that you *and your father* knew that your mother appreciated his style and his ideas about parenting. Her positive feelings build his confidence as a parent and motivate him to be even more involved in your life. And her

Mom's Opinions: What Kind of Parent Is Dad?

What did you think your mother felt as you were growing up? In addressing these statements, use 0 to mean "never or rarely," 1 to mean "most of the time," and 2 to mean "almost always."

____ Your father is just as approachable and sweet-hearted as I am.

____ I want you to talk to your dad as much as you talk to me about personal things.

____ Your dad has sacrificed and contributed as much as I have to you kids.

____ You and your dad need to be just as close as you and I are.

____ Your father is as wise and insightful as I am.

____ Your father is just as sympathetic and understanding as I am.

____ You and your dad need to spend just as much time alone as you and I do.

____ You ought to have private conversations with your dad without me around.

____ Your father's way of disciplining you is just as good as mine.

____ Your father enjoys being a parent as much as I do.

____ Score (20 possible)

positive feelings help you to value your father's ideas and his style of parenting even when they aren't exactly like your mother's. Millions of mothers can be congratulated for having done an exceptional job at this. On the other hand, the lower her score, the more likely you are to have grown up believing that your father is inferior to your mother as a parent. Because she considered herself the child-raising expert, you too came to believe that she was right and dad was wrong whenever they disagreed about how to raise you. This not only leads you to think less of your dad's skills and ideas as a parent, but it also leads *him* to feel incompetent, inferior, or unwelcome: "If my wife criticizes, mocks, or disagrees so often with my ideas or the way I relate to our kids, then I guess I'd better back away, keep quiet, and yield to her ideas. I guess what I've been told is right after all: Women are wiser and better parents than men." In other words, it is not good for your father-daughter relationships if your mother was driving the parent train—allowing your dad into the engine room with her every now and then to toot the whistle.

A high score also means that you rarely encountered these two situations that detract from father-daughter relationships: First, "Just wait until your father gets home!" If most of the discipline was left up to your father, you may have come to believe that he was too judgmental, too strict, or too unsympathetic compared with your mother. You may have grown to fear him or to become overly anxious about his finding out about your mistakes. Second, "Let's not let your father find out about *this* because he will be so angry (or so disappointed in you or so hurt)." *This* may be something as trivial as your getting into trouble at school for not doing your homework. Or *this* may be something more significant, such as your mom discovering that you're on birth control as a teenager. But by agreeing that the two of you will hide *this* from your father, your mother is creating an impression of your father that can detract from your relationship with him—that *she* can be trusted, that *she* can deal with or forgive what you have done, and that *she* will love you and be proud of you despite your flaws, *but that your father cannot do these things.* It may be true that your father would be more upset than your mother. But how will you ever know because you've already judged him and refused to give him a chance to show you how he would respond. If your mother got a high score on the quiz, she did not create an alliance with you behind your father's back—an alliance based on the assumption that dad is the "bad guy" who can't be as forgiving, as understanding, or as reasonable as mom.

Generally speaking, men and women do interact differently with their children and have different ideas about the "right" way to raise children. And this is why it's so important that your mother never make you feel that her ways are better than your father's. If they are like most parents in our country, your father was more likely than your mother to nurture and to guide you in the following ways: [2,21]

- Pointing out how you could do something a better way

- Challenging or stretching you intellectually

- Discouraging you from whining and feeling sorry for yourself

- Focusing more on solving your problems than on complaining about them

- Teaching you to be more self-disciplined and more self-reliant

- Refusing to give you too much power over the adults

- Teaching you to take responsibility for your own mistakes

- Encouraging you to try new or difficult things

- Discussing serious things with you such as school, finances, and your future job

- Encouraging you to try again after failing at something

- Teaching you to set realistic goals instead of fantasizing

So let's consider one example of how a mother can strengthen the father-daughter relationship by showing her daughter that dad's ways of parenting are just as good as mom's. Let's assume that you are 14 years old and have just had a big argument with your closest girlfriend, Sue. Odds are that you would go to your mother first because you automatically assume that she will have better advice or be more comforting than your father. As we've already discussed in Chapter 3, men and women are trained to respond and to communicate differently when they're trying to help or to comfort the people they love. This means that your dad probably will jump more quickly than your mom will into giving you ideas for how to fix your problem with Sue. So let's assume that you then complain to your mom that your dad isn't sympathetic enough. At this point she has the chance to help you to appreciate your father's way of helping and comforting you even though they aren't the same as hers. She might say something like: "Your father is a sympathetic, understanding person who loves you so much that he wants to help you fix things with Sue as quickly as possible. He has good ideas, so take advantage of his advice." However she does it, your mother strengthens your father-daughter relationship by continually pointing out that just because your dad and she relate to you differently, *her way isn't better than his.*

Your Parents' Marriage: Fairness and Power

As you were growing up, how did you feel about your father in terms of his doing his fair share of the work at home? Did you feel that he treated your mother fairly and equitably? Did they seem to have a fair arrangement for raising you kids and running the household? Even if your parents had a happy marriage, you may have had some negative feelings about your father not treating your mother fairly enough. Especially if your mom was a housewife, you may have felt that your father didn't do his fair share at home—or that he didn't appreciate her enough. From your viewpoint as a child, it may have seemed that your father wasn't doing his fair share. If you've ever felt this way, taking a closer look at the following realities probably will leave you with a more sympathetic, more balanced view of your father.

First, much of the work that fathers do around the home may go unnoticed by their children. A traditional mother's contributions are usually very obvious and visible: cooking, cleaning, laundering, vacuuming, grocery shopping, taking care of pets, taking care of sick children, preparing birthday parties, and taxiing you kids around. But the kind of work a father traditionally does is not as apparent or as visible to most children: shopping for, repairing, assembling, installing, cleaning, and maintaining things—cars, computers, tools, appliances, toys, pools, outdoor lighting, barbeque grills; doing yard work, shoveling snow, or any activity involving physical risk (climbing ladders, cleaning gutters, moving furniture, or repairing the roof); handling the family's finances (health and car insurance, taxes, investments); replacing heat and air conditioning filters and cleaning basements and attics; coaching and attending children's sports events; building fires; disposing of garbage; and remodeling, painting, rewiring, and unplugging drains. There's a good chance that your dad was doing his fair share even though you thought he was slouching off or exploiting your mom. So unless your father truly didn't do his fair share, hopefully your mother never gave you the impression that he was taking advantage of her when it came to running the home and raising you kids.

Second, most of us have gotten the impression from the media—and even from college textbooks—that employed mothers work a "second shift" providing childcare and doing work around the house while the fathers are relaxing and enjoying their free time after they get home from work. As the popular saying puts it: "A man works from rising to setting sun, but a woman's work is *never* done." Yet, as we discussed in Chapter 2 and as you can see from the "Eye Openers" below, most employed men also have a "second shift" of household chores and child-care responsibilities. If you

Eye Openers[8-13]

- When both parents work equal numbers of hours outside the home, they spend almost equal time with the children and doing household tasks.
- The more hours the mother works and the higher her income, the more time the father generally spends with the children.
- Employed fathers are just as stressed as employed mothers trying to balance work and family.
- In only 20 percent of families does the mother have more financial responsibility than the father because she earns the larger salary.
- Counting the hours spent commuting, working, doing house and yard work, and taking care of kids, the average man has 5 hours *less* free time each week than the average woman.
- Compared with mothers' jobs, fathers' jobs usually require longer hours, more traveling, more commuting, and fewer options to work part time or to quit work for several years.

believed as you were growing up that employed women were always doing way more than their fair share at home, you would be less likely to notice your father's contributions at home. Remember, what you believe about any group of people (such as fathers or mothers) influences what you "see" and what you remember *even when your beliefs are not true.* You see and remember those things about your father that you have been prepared ahead of time to believe about fathers. Now that you're an adult, take a close look at the eye-opening facts about the vast majority of fathers in our country—and use these facts to reconsider any negative feelings you may have about how fair your father was to your mother. As you look back at your family, ask yourself: Have I misjudged my father by assuming that he was taking advantage of my mother by not doing his fair share at home? And keep these eye-opening statistics in mind.

Your Parents' Marriage: How Happy?

During most of the time you were growing up, how happy did your parents seem with each other? Did you see them as joyful and loving? Did you think that your dad was a good husband, or did your mother often seem to be disappointed or unhappy with him? Thinking back to your childhood, how would you describe the way your mother felt about your father? Use the following checklist to help you travel back in time.

My Dad as a Husband

What did your mother think of your father as a husband while you were growing up? In addressing these issues, use 0 to mean "rarely," 1 to mean "half the time," and 2 to mean "almost always."

As a husband, my father was(is)

___ loving.

___ communicative.

___ thoughtful/considerate.

(Continued)

_____ attentive.

_____ playful.

_____ appreciative/complimentary.

_____ loyal/trustworthy.

_____ comforting/nurturing.

_____ forgiving.

_____ nonjudgmental/accepting.

_____ unselfish/giving.

_____ generous.

_____ fair/reasonable.

_____ sympathetic/understanding.

_____ supportive/encouraging.

_____ Score (30 possible)

For the sake of your father-daughter relationship, let's hope that your parents were happily married. If they were not satisfied with their relationship, there are four ways that your relationship with your dad is usually damaged.[13,22]

First, you become your mother's confidante, comforter, and advisor. She pulls you into their marital conflicts or talks to you about things that he's done in the past that upset her. She points out his weaknesses as a husband or as a father. She tells you things about him that he would be embarrassed or humiliated by your knowing. She criticizes or makes fun of him—sometimes in front of you. She turns to you for sympathy and comfort, as if you were her best friend instead of her child. Not surprisingly, you often end up siding with her against your father, adopting her negative feelings about him, or feeling deeply disappointed in or angry at your father.

Second, you become so involved in your mother's life that you become like one person—enmeshed. When a parent and child become so overly involved and overly dependent on each other that they start behaving almost as if they were one person, psychologists refer to them as *enmeshed.* If you're enmeshed, you absorb whatever negative beliefs and feelings your mother has about your father. You often treat him like she does, seeing him through her eyes instead of your own. You also feel that you're responsible for making your mother happy, helping to solve her problems, or standing up for her or taking her side against your dad. You may feel guilty about leaving home or moving too far away from her. It's almost as if you've become her parent—which is why we psychologists say you have a *role reversal.* The following quiz can help you to see whether you've become overly involved or enmeshed with either of your parents.

Are You and Your Mother Too Involved?

As you were growing up, how did you feel about your mother? In addressing these statements, use 0 to mean "never," 1 to mean "seldom," 2 to mean "fairly often," and 3 to mean "almost always."

____ I have a hard time saying no to her.

____ I feel that it's my responsibility to make her happier.

____ I can't enjoy my own happiness when she's unhappy.

____ I feel that it's my responsibility to help her solve problems in her life.

____ I feel selfish or guilty when I ask her to give up something for me.

____ I give up doing things in order to make her happy.

____ I feel like her counselor, advisor, or best friend.

____ I think that she is really lonely or sad.

____ I worry about what's going to happen to her in the future.

____ I pity or feel sorry for her.

____ Score (30 possible)

The higher your score, the more overly involved or enmeshed you are with your mom. This is not good for your father-daughter relationship. Not only might you end up blaming him for her unhappiness, you also may resent him for not being your mother's best friend and helpmate. Because you feel the need to advise and protect her, you tend to take on too many of her negative views of your father.

Third, if your mother isn't happy with your dad, you are likely to pick up some of her negative feelings about him. You're likely to feel about your father the way these daughters do: "Mom points out his flaws in front of me, which makes my father and me uncomfortable around each other." "My mom is constantly putting him down for small things she doesn't like about him. I have taken on a nagging tone with him too. I know he hates the way we talk to him like a child." "I wish she would stop telling me about their fights. But she accuses me of not caring about her when I refuse to listen to her complain about dad." "The hostile things she tells me about dad stick in my mind for much longer than a few hours. I take to heart everything she says and find myself resenting my dad." "My mom doesn't have many friends, so she's always told me and my sister about her arguments with dad. It makes it very difficult to see him from my own perspective."

Fourth, your father becomes less involved with you. Sensing that you're hearing a lot of negative things about him from your mother, he feels more uncomfortable around you. He feels that your mother and you have ganged up on him. Feeling that you have sided against him, he spends less time with you—which, in turn, makes you feel less loved. So there's a vicious cycle: He feels less loved by you, so he draws further back, which makes you feel less loved by him, so you pull further back, which then makes him feel even more unloved, and on and on.

Adultery

As far as your parents' marriage is concerned, your father-daughter bond is most damaged if your mother tells you—or leads you to believe—that your father cheated on her. Although most parents no doubt realize that it's wrong to share this kind of intimate information with their children,

Eye Openers

- Mothers are more likely than fathers to become enmeshed or overly dependent on their children.[7,22]
- A mother is more likely to become enmeshed with a child who has a chronic illness such as asthma or epilepsy.[12]
- When only a few years old, children can become so enmeshed with their mothers that they form a long-standing pattern of aligning with them against their fathers.[9,22]
- As she is growing up, a daughter has a better relationship with her father when her mother does not rely on her for advice or comfort on adult issues—especially issues involving the parents' relationship with each other.[6]
- When parents are unhappy with each other, most children side with their mothers against their fathers.[23,24]
- When parents are unhappily married, the mother generally becomes overly involved and overly dependent on the children, and the father generally becomes more distant and withdrawn.[9,13]
- A child's relationship with the father is more troubled or distant when the mother is chronically unhappy or clinically depressed.[25]

in moments of anger, pain, or jealousy they too often do let the children know. If you've been in this situation yourself, you already know how much damage this does to your relationship with your unfaithful parent.

If in your family it was your father who cheated, be sure you don't jump to the conclusion that men are almost always the unfaithful ones. The reality is that nowadays women are almost as likely as men to commit adultery. Women are also more likely than men to end their marriage because they have fallen in love with someone else. That is, a father who has an affair is less likely than a mother who has an affair to ask for a divorce.[26] While it is easy to assume that it is only the sexy-looking or liberal mom with a career who cheats, wholesome-looking, conservative housewives also have affairs and dump their faithful husband for other men.[27] Moreover, wives in their twenties are *more likely* to cheat than their husbands.[28] What these statistics mean for your father-daughter relationship is this: Don't automatically assume that if one of your parents cheated, it was your dad "because he's a man and that's how men are." And don't automatically assume that just because your father seemed to be the sexier or the more liberal parent—or the parent with the most status or excitement at work away from home—that he was the one who cheated.

Now, if you do know for sure that your father had an affair, what can you do to minimize the damage to your relationship with him? First, keep this in mind: Through the media and through our general assumptions about men and adultery, you have been encouraged to see your father's affair in the worst possible light. In contrast, if you find out that your mother had an affair, you have been primed to be more understanding and more forgiving. In other words, your father probably will pay a bigger price than your mother does for the same mistake.

Let me give you just three examples of this bias again men who have affairs. In the popular movie *Terms of Endearment,* the mother (pregnant with her third child) discovers that her husband is having an affair with a pretty, young college student. With baby in arms, the mother literally chases her husband's mistress across the campus to confront her. The mother also has an affair—but her husband never finds out, so no real damage is done. Besides, her lover is a sweet, plain-looking, middle-aged guy whose wife won't have sex with him anymore because she has a bad back. You just can't help but like this guy. We can't be too angry at this unfaithful mother because we discover that she has terminal cancer. As she is dying, she *and* her husband agree that he is too immature to raise their kids—*largely because he had an affair.* Then there is the mother in the wildly popular movie and book *The Bridges of Madison County.* She falls in love with a total stranger in three days while her good-natured but boring husband is away with their two teenage kids at a farmers' convention. The mother is a self-sacrificing, exhausted, lonely housewife. We're supposed to sympathize with her situation out there in the middle of nowhere on the farm. Then this sensitive, lonely man pops into her life while he's photographing old bridges—not a young man, not a man she's been flirting with at work. The love of her life magically appears at her doorstep—a coincidence, fate, destiny, something that's "meant to be." Their affair is loving, romantic, and tender. In the end, being the good person she is, she "sacrifices" by staying with her family. Many years later after she has died, her adult children find out about her affair. Not only do they forgive her, but they also admire her for staying with their family. Now consider the father who has an affair in *Fatal Attraction.* His mentally deranged, sexy mistress tries to kill his wife, kidnaps his daughter, and boils the family's pet bunny to death in a pasta pot in their own kitchen. In film after film, TV show after TV show, the father who commits adultery comes off looking far worse than the mother who cheats.[29]

What all this means is that if you find out that your father cheated, you assume the worst. Regardless of what the circumstances actually were, you probably will be less forgiving and less sympathetic than if you find out that your mother cheated. We want to find ways to forgive the unfaithful mother because she is, after all, a mother. We want to understand *why* she cheated. We want to hear her side of the story *before* condemning her too harshly. We're more likely to forgive mothers than fathers because we tell ourselves: She couldn't help it. It was more about love than sex. She was lonely, misunderstood, or unappreciated by her husband. She had a "meaningful" relationship with a nice guy, not a shallow, sleazy sexual fling like a father might have. We assume that mother had a forgivable reason for doing what she did—and we're willing to listen to it. Unfortunately for our father-daughter relationships, most of us are not willing to give our fathers this same break. One way of helping your relationship is to ask yourself the following: If it had been my mother who cheated, would I have treated her *exactly* the same way I have treated my father? Would I have been more forgiving or more willing to consider the circumstances that caused my parent to cheat?

Something else that might diminish the damage to your relationship with your dad is to ask yourself this: When a spouse cheats, who is it that has been betrayed? Whose sexual and emotional relationship is at stake? Whose relationship is adultery about? Most daughters tell me that their father "betrayed the family" or that "I can't trust him any more because of what he did." If this is how you feel, I ask you to consider this: When two adults enter a serious relationship or get married, they make an agreement about what kind of sexual arrangement they want to have. Are they going to have sex only with each other? Or are they going to occasionally have sex with someone else? Are they going to be honest with each other or just agree to "do what you want but don't let me find out and I'll do the same." Are they going to have children together, continue to live together to raise their kids, and agree to lead private sexual lives because one or both of them is not heterosexual? Parents make all sorts of different agreements along these lines. So my point is this: Adultery is not about the relationship between parent and child. It is about the relationship or agreement between the two parents. I'm not saying that children don't get hurt when their parents tell them about adultery. I'm saying that when your parent cheats, he or she has violated a promise he or she made to his or her spouse, not a promise he or she made to you. *An unfaithful parent has not cheated or betrayed you.*

Another way to think about adultery is this: If your parent is a wonderful parent to you, why should you punish him or her for being a "bad" or imperfect spouse? If your parent has a problem such as alcoholism, a propensity toward physical violence, or mental illness, it *is* your business because their problem has a direct impact on the way that parent treats *you on a regular basis.* But cheating on a spouse does not mean that the person is mistreating or ignoring his or her children. Don't get me wrong. I am not defending adultery. Nor am I saying that an unfaithful spouse shouldn't pay a price. What I am saying is that the punishing and the forgiving should be between the spouses.

Even when it's your mother who cheated, you can end up having bad feelings toward your father. Daughters in this situation have told me that they resent their father for being too weak to divorce their mother. If not by divorcing her, these daughters feel that their fathers are not making their mother pay a price of any kind for what she did. Others lose respect for their father because they feel that he has let their mother take advantage of him in many others ways as well. These daughters see their fathers as weak men who have allowed their wives to dominate the family and to mistreat them as husbands. Some also blame their father for their mother's affair: "He worked so much that she had to turn to another man for attention." "If he hadn't been so insensitive, she wouldn't have had to do what she did."

What Now?

Even though you may have acquired some of your mother's negative ideas about your father as a parent, it's not too late to change them. First, you can start spending a lot more time alone with your father. Using the ideas we discussed for getting to know him, try to see him through your own eyes rather than through your mother's. Grant him the freedom to relate to you the way he would like without your mother around. Your mother may not feel comfortable with this, since you and your dad haven't spent lots of time alone. If she says anything to you, tell her directly that you are going to be spending more time alone with your father because you want to get to know him better. When you're home visiting, you can go for long walks with him or go off for hours for coffee. Do whatever it takes to get your father away from the house and alone with you.

Second, thank your father for the things you realize he did right as a parent. Look back at the list of things that fathers typically do better than mothers. Talk to him about how you benefited from what he did for you. If you can, apologize to him for being so critical of him as a parent when you were younger. For example, if you used to criticize him for "pushing" you too hard, maybe now you can compliment him for having encouraged, expanded, and widened your visions and your skills. Or if you used to tell him he wasn't understanding or supportive like your mother was, maybe now you can tell him that you recognize that he was being understanding and supportive in his own ways. Let him know that many of his ideas and techniques for raising children are valuable. If you have children yourself, ask for his advice from time to time. Do whatever you can to make him feel that his ideas are welcomed and appreciated.

Third, if your mother criticizes or ridicules your father in front of you, or if she confides in you about their marital problems, tell her to stop. Without using an angry voice, let her know that even though you have done this for years, you are no longer willing to be her advisor or her confidante. In a calm voice, tell her that if she has serious problems with your father, you'd be proud of her if she would go see a therapist. You might say something like this: "Mom, for years you have let me know what you don't like about dad as a father and as a husband. I love you and I care about your happiness. I also love my father. As I age, I want a relationship with each of you that is entirely separate from how you feel about each other. If you're this unhappy with dad, why not see a therapist? If not, talk to some of your friends instead of to me. I don't feel comfortable anymore hearing these things from you. I don't feel close to you when you criticize him in front of me. I don't feel that it's good for my relationship with you when you to tell me negative things about him. I'm sure you can find someone else to confide it because I won't be doing this anymore."

Finally, stop judging your father's way of parenting you as "not right" or "not good enough" just because he doesn't relate to you exactly the way your mother does. Stop assuming that a woman's way of relating to children is always the best way. Open your eyes to your father's talents, insights, and wisdom as a parent. Allow him to be a parent in his own way rather than wanting him to be the clone of your mother. Stop comparing him in negative ways with your mother—or with other female parents. You wouldn't like it if people at work or at school were constantly criticizing your way of doing things just because you didn't approach your work the way the men did, now would you? I'll bet you'd also be annoyed and discouraged if the men at work treated you as if you had to defend your "woman's way" of doing things because most of them, as men, were the experts on how the job should be done the "right" way. Give your dad a break. Stop asking him to do the job of parenting the way your mother does it. Grant him the freedom to be a unique parent, not a replica of your mother. Celebrate the fact that he doesn't relate to you the way most female parents would. Embrace him, and embrace the many gifts he has to offer you as your male parent.

Chapter 6

Sex
Let's Stop Pretending

- Do you deceive your father when it comes to your sexual or romantic life?

- Do you feel uneasy when sexual topics are mentioned around you and your father?

- Have issues related to sex, dating, or marriage created tension between you and your father?

- Is your dad disappointed in your sexual values or your lifestyle?

If so, this chapter is designed for you. If you and your father are like most daughters and fathers, issues such as these at some time have put a strain on your relationship: When is a daughter old enough to date and to make wise sexual decisions? How honest should fathers and daughters be about their sexual beliefs and experiences? What role should a father play as his daughter starts dating and maturing sexually? What if the daughter is having sex or living with her boyfriend when she knows that her father would be upset if he found out? What if the father disapproves of the person his daughter is dating or marrying? What if the father disapproves of his daughter's beliefs about interracial dating, gay or lesbian relationships, or terminating unwanted pregnancies?

In terms of sex and relationships, I've found that most of the bad feelings or misunderstandings between fathers and daughters stem from five situations: (1) You or your father is making the wrong assumptions about the other's beliefs. (2) You don't understand your father's feelings and fears. (3) You don't see your father as your ally and advisor, so you aren't honest or open enough with him. (4) You are not confident or comfortable enough with your own beliefs and decisions. (5) You haven't figured out how to handle whatever differences the two of you have about sexual issues or lifestyles.

As a result of these five circumstances, you end up afraid or uncomfortable talking to one another about anything having to do with sex or romantic relationships. You don't go to your father for advice or let him know anything about what's going on in your private life. You're probably uncomfortable around each other whenever topics related to sex or romantic relationships arise. You probably pretend to be someone you're not by hiding the truth about your beliefs and your lifestyle from your father. You're afraid to let him know who you are. And none of this is good for your father-daughter relationship.

Don't get me wrong. I'm *not* saying that you and your father should share the details of your sexual lives with each other. And I'm not saying that either of you has to give up your privacy. Remember what we discussed in Chapter 3. There's a big difference between *privacy* and secrecy, lies, and deception. Both you and your father need and deserve privacy—and privacy doesn't damage relationships. What damages relationships is deception and dishonesty. Lying about who you are and what you believe is different from maintaining your privacy. For example, if you're having sex, living with your boyfriend, or dating someone of another race, you're being dishonest and deceptive to lead your father to believe that you're a virgin who disapproves of interracial dating. Or if, as an adult, you're hiding the fact that you're gay from your father, you're being dishonest about a very fundamental part of your life. Neither you nor your father should be pretending to be someone you aren't just because you think that the other disapproves. My aim is to help you to be more honest and more relaxed with your father when it comes to what's going on in your personal life—to help you stop lying to him about who you are or what you believe in regard to sex and romantic relationships.

One final point: Most of what I'm going to be talking about refers to daughters past high school age. Until you reach the age of 18, by law, you are still your father's financial responsibility. Whatever sexual decisions you make can have a direct financial and legal impact on *his* life. But once you've turned 18, you're legally responsible for yourself. Your father is no longer held responsible for any decisions you make about sex and relationships. Now the consequences are solely yours. So let's look at five areas that generally have the most impact on your father-daughter relationship.

Sexual Beliefs: Yours and Your Father's

How much do you really know about your father's beliefs regarding sex and relationships? How much do you know about his sexual or romantic life as a teenager or young man? How many hours have you spent with him talking about his beliefs and his past—and talking privately without anyone else around? If you're like most of the daughters I know, you make many assumptions about your father without ever having talked to him about these things. You may be assuming that your father is much more conservative than he really is. Without ever having talked to him about these matters, have you jumped to the conclusion that he disapproves of premarital sex, couples living together before marriage, or couples deciding not to have children? Do you have a hard time imagining him ever having done the sexual or romantic things that you have done? Do you assume that he has never gotten into trouble or never regretted doing certain sexual things like you have? Do you think that he's always been the naive, saintly person, and that you're the experienced, naughty one? Well, let's start by seeing just how much you know about most men your father's age.

Your Father's Generation

What do you believe is *true* about most men now between the ages of 45 and 60?

____ Most were virgins when they got married.

____ Most have been married only once.

____ Most waited until their twenties to have sex for the first time.

____ Most married a virgin.

____ Most disapprove of people having sex before marriage.

____ Most never drank or smoked cigarettes as teenagers.

____ Most never used any illegal drug.

____ Most oppose sex education in the schools.

____ Most want abortion made illegal again.

____ Most believe that interracial marriages should be outlawed again.

____ Score (10 possible trues)

132 EMBRACING YOUR FATHER

What's your score? The correct answer is zero. Not one of these statements is true.[1-3] Most men your father's age were not sexually or socially conservative—and neither were the women they dated and married. Only 10 percent of the men and 15 percent of the women in your parents' age group were virgins when they married. Nearly 80 percent were having sex, drinking, smoking, and trying drugs as teenagers. More than half have been divorced at least once, and another 20 percent had children without ever getting married. Nearly a third of the women were already pregnant when the couple got married. Most men had three or four lovers before marriage, and most women had more than one. Interracial and interfaith marriages increased dramatically in your father's generation. Your legal rights to have an abortion, to marry someone of another race, to keep your job if you're gay, and to possess small amounts of recreational drugs without being sent to jail exist because *his* generation, *not* yours, created more liberal laws. In short, there's not as much difference as you might think between your generation and his. So consider the facts before assuming that your father is going to be upset or disapprove of what you or your friends are doing.

But why does it matter what you assume about your father's beliefs? Even if you are wrong about what he believes, how does it hurt your relationship with him? Well, to begin with, if you're assuming that he's a lot more conservative than you are, you probably feel tense and uncomfortable around him when you don't need to. You might be hiding things from him or pretending to be someone you're not when, in fact, he might not disapprove because he or his friends did the same sorts of things that you're doing. I'm not saying that your dad is necessarily going to have the same views that you do. I'm just saying that you shouldn't presume that he is more conservative than you just because he's your father—or just because you can't imagine him being a sexual, romantic young man.

When I convince daughters to talk with their fathers about their experiences and opinions, many are pleasantly surprised and relieved to discover that their fathers have done such things as skinny dipping, living with their girlfriends, hitchhiking across country with a lover, smoking marijuana, and making foolish mistakes in their relationships. If you discover that your father isn't as perfect or as conservative as you imagined, you'll probably feel more relaxed sharing your own beliefs and behavior with him. If it turns out that your dad is much more conservative than you and that he does—or would—disapprove of your lifestyle and beliefs, we'll see how to handle your differences later in this chapter. For now, I'm just inviting you to take the first step by finding out for yourself what your father really believes. You can start by asking him questions such as the ones in the following box. Give him a break by allowing him the chance to share his beliefs with you. Remember, nobody else should be around while the two of you are talking. This discussion is just between you and your father.

Sex: Dad's Opinions and Experiences

1. What were the best and the worst dating experiences you had before your got married?
2. How do you feel about people living together or having sex before marriage? Why?
3. How do you feel about gay and lesbian relationships?
4. What girlfriends had the greatest impact on you? How?
5. What do you wish had been different about your first romantic experiences?
6. How do you feel about sex education and contraceptives for teenagers?
7. How have your ideas about love, dating, marriage, and sex changed from the time you were a teenager?
8. What are your greatest sexual fears for young people today?
9. How do you feel about people getting married because the woman is pregnant?
10. What were your greatest worries for me when I started dating?
11. What were the most heart-breaking experiences you had with women in your life?
12. When did you feel foolish or awkward with women?
13. What do you wish you had known before you had your first serious girlfriend?
14. What do you wish you had known about sex and love as a young man?
15. How liberal or conservative do you think you are about social or sexual issues? Why?

Your Father's Fears

How did your father react to your dating and your romantic partners? Was dating a source of tension, or did it bring you and your father closer? Why might you and your father have had more problems once you started dating? All these questions probably can be answered with one word—*fear*. Your father was afraid of what might happen to you or afraid of the ways in which you seemed to be changing yourself in order to please the person you were dating. Let's take a look at what his fears may have been.

When you first got interested in boys, your father knew things that you didn't know—things that frightened him. And if he knew or suspected that you were not heterosexual, he probably was afraid that certain people or family members might mistreat, hurt, or discriminate against you. If he himself felt uncomfortable with your sexual orientation, he probably feared that your father-daughter relationship might be damaged as well. As a younger person who wasn't fully aware of his fears, you couldn't understand that the way he reacted to you was based on his love and concern for you—or based on his own confusion and discomfort with your sexual orientation. You may have felt that he was trying to control you, to criticize you, or to keep you from having fun. Meanwhile, he was probably trying to protect or to guide you. Especially if you started your teenage years believing that fathers are uptight and unhappy about their daughters' dating, you probably couldn't see that your father was, quite simply, afraid. Thinking back to when you first started dating, how would you have answered the questions in the following quiz? How many of these fears did your father probably have back then?

What is your score? The perfect score is 15. All the statements are true. [2-5] Unless you were fully aware of all these facts when you started dating, however, you probably felt that your father was trying to control you, to interfere with your personal life, and to criticize your judgment when he was trying to protect and educate you. On the other hand, your father may not have been aware of these facts. He may have been assuming a lot of negative, scary things about teenagers that aren't in fact true. For example, if he believed that most teenagers have sex with lots of different people without using contraceptives, he was probably too strict and too suspicious of what you and your friends were doing. And that's not good for your relationship with him. But if your father realized that most young people

Your Father's Fears: Sexual Facts

Which do you believe are true for most teenage and young adult daughters? Which do you think your father believed were true when you were a teenager?

____ Many teenage girls feel they were pressured into having sex before they felt old enough.

____ Females usually date or marry men from backgrounds similar to theirs.

____ One-fourth of young women have been pregnant before they turn 18.

____ Teenage girls usually use birth control.

____ Females are more likely to be raped when they've been drinking heavily.

____ Most rape victims are raped by a man they know.

____ Most women only have one or two sexual partners before they marry.

____ Girls are most likely to get raped as teenagers.

____ Most girls have sex before they are 20.

____ Only 1 in 10 women is a virgin when she marries.

____ Most teenagers have sex with someone they're in a serious, long-term relationship with.

____ Girls who mature early are more likely than later maturing girls to get pregnant.

____ Most girls from religious, conservative families have sex before marriage.

____ Most teenagers get information about contraception from their peers, not from adults.

____ Most teenagers have sex without using condoms.

____ Girls who attend college are the most likely to abort an unwanted pregnancy.

____ Your score (15 possible trues)

do not have sex casually with people they hardly know or get pregnant because they aren't using contraceptives, he was probably more relaxed when you started dating.

Your father also probably feared your being hurt because you had such naive ideas about sex and love. Most teenage girls have very unrealistic, overly romantic ideas about love and sex—ideas that lead us to make some very bad decisions in our sexual and social lives.[6,7] Like most teenage girls, you may have been easily swept off your feet by charming, good-looking, popular guys—ignoring the "nice" guys because they didn't measure up to your romanticized ideas. Even though these nice guys treated you the best and brought out the best in you, you weren't very interested in dating them because they weren't exciting or romantic enough for you. You may have dated some boys who weren't very good for you—or very good to you. Meanwhile, your father knew that males are not princes and females are not princesses. He knew that the most charming, exciting people are often not the best people to date or marry. As you think back now to some of your decisions, you'd have to agree that "love is blind." But your father wasn't blind, so he tried to advise or warn you about some of those choices you were making. Unfortunately, you felt that he was criticizing you, treating you like a child, or not trusting your judgment. Especially if your mother never said anything negative about any of your boyfriends, you probably thought that your dad was judgmental, unsupportive, and critical.

Chances are your father also feared losing you. I don't mean losing you because you were spending more time with boyfriends. And I don't mean losing you in the sense that someday you would leave home and create a life with a husband. By "losing you" I mean that when you dated certain boys, your father saw that *your personality and your essence were being lost—you were disappearing in the relationship.* You were losing your own self. You were shrinking into *less*—less self-reliant, less self-confident, less outgoing, less mature, less energetic, and less physically healthy. Your personality, your dreams, and your ideas were shriveling instead of expanding. You were becoming more of a little girl and less of a woman—giving up your own goals, sacrificing what was best for you, ignoring your own needs, and pretending to be someone other than who you always had been in order to make this particular boyfriend happy. The you that you were becoming with certain boyfriends was a tense, withdrawn, dependent, passive, timid, joyless, intimidated, and self-demeaning copy of the you that your father and friends had always known. Your father also saw that in that relationship you were afraid to be you—afraid to disagree, afraid to speak your mind, afraid to do things on your own, afraid to pursue your own dreams, and afraid of not being good enough in some way. It's *not* that your father disliked that particular boyfriend. He disliked what was being lost of you in that relationship. All the while, you wanted your father to approve of the person you were dating. But he couldn't because he saw that *you* were disappearing—and he feared that you might lose your self permanently.

Thinking about all the things a father might fear, look back at how your father treated you and your boyfriends. Try to remember exactly how you felt about your father at the time you started dating or becoming sexually active. Now ask yourself: What was my dad probably afraid of at the time? What was he worried might happen to me? How do I wish he had let me know what he was afraid of? How did his fears change our relationship? What could I have done differently so that my father would not have been so afraid? Am I still angry or hurt about the way dad treated me or any of my boyfriends? If I am, why haven't I talked to him and asked him what was going on in his mind at the time?

Dad and My Boyfriends

What three situations involving my romantic life have created tension between me and my father?

1. _____
2. _____
3. _____

What do I wish dad had done in each of these situations?

1. _____
2. _____
3. _____

(*Continued*)

What could I have done differently to make my father feel better?

1. _____

2. _____

3. _____

Why do I think my father acted the way he did in each situation?

1. _____

2. _____

3. _____

What were my father's greatest worries or fears for me while I was dating?

1. _____

2. _____

3. _____

Father as Advisor and Ally

Remember what we discussed in Chapter 1. What you believe and expect from fathers affects how you treat your own dad—even when your beliefs and expectations are not true. Here are some of the beliefs that can cause you to distance yourself from your father once you start dating: Fathers aren't interested in talking to their daughters about personal things such as love, sex, marriage, or romance. Fathers don't want to know anything about their daughters' personal lives. Fathers don't like their daughters' boyfriends because they don't' want their daughters to grow up. Fathers don't have much insight or wisdom when it comes to helping their daughters with anything related to sex, romance, or love. A father can't be as helpful as a mother giving a daughter advice about male-female relationships.

Negative beliefs like these make it difficult for you to treat your father as your advisor and ally. In fact, insulting beliefs like these lead you to distance yourself from your father because you think he can't understand or isn't interested in what you're going through. On the other hand, maybe you're one of those lucky daughters who started out with positive beliefs about fathers. Maybe, like the following young adult daughters, you have always given your father the chance to know you and to be your friend instead of shutting him out: "I've always gone to my dad when I needed to talk about sex or relationships." "A few weeks ago my dad sent me an e-mail about how I need to change the way I communicate with my fiancé. He's always been helpful that way." "My dad has always been relaxed and open with me about sex. And because he's comfortable, I enjoy talking with him." "My dad is the one who helped me realize that I was in a dead end relationship. I always go to him for advice." "My dad talked to all us girls about sex, birth control, tampons, having our periods—all of it. At first, I was a little embarrassed; but I'm glad he did. I expect my future husband to do the same for our daughters." "When I was getting out of a long-term relationship, my dad wrote me this letter that put everything in perspective, and he called several times a week just to let me talk about it." "Dad always gives me good advice about my boyfriends from the guy perspective—after all, he can fill me in on all the secret stuff about men!"

If you've never felt like this about your father, it's not too late to begin treating him like your ally and advisor. But how do you start? Well, first, let's figure out why you have shut your father out of your personal life and why you may be less than truthful with him. Are you afraid you'll disappoint or anger him—or afraid that he'll be ashamed of you? Regardless of your age, do you need him to see you as a sexless, innocent little girl instead of as a woman? If so, why? Do you think he's going to make fun of you for asking questions or trying to talk about such things as sex, love, and marriage? Do you think that you're going to embarrass him? Maybe you haven't stopped to ask yourself why you're afraid or uncomfortable with the idea of talking to him about these things. So try the following quiz to get focused on your fears.

Honesty: Why or Why Not?

Why haven't you been more open with your father about your sexual or romantic life?

1. _____
2. _____
3. _____

(Continued)

What do you fear losing if you are more honest with him?

1. _____

2. _____

3. _____

What would your father have to do to make it easier for you to be more honest or more relaxed talking with him about relationships?

1. _____

2. _____

3. _____

Your Lack of Confidence

I've found that the daughter who desperately wants her father to approve of her sexual or romantic decisions is the one who has the least confidence about her own choices. Because she isn't very confident or convinced that what she's doing is right for her, she wants her father to vote for it. For example, if you decide to get married but your father doesn't seem very enthusiastic, you're probably a lot more upset with him if you yourself have doubts. But when you're 100 percent certain that what you're doing is right for you, you're less dependent on needing your father's approval. Sure you'd like everyone you know to approve of every decision you make. You'd like everyone to say that it's fine that you're marrying a man of a different faith or that you and your boyfriend have moved in together. And wouldn't it be dandy if your father were thrilled when you told him that you and your female partner are going to get married in his church by his minister? But let's get real. Everyone isn't always going to approve of your decisions—not even those who love you most, like your father. So in situations where you're really upset or disappointed in him for disapproving of a decision you've made, ask yourself: Am I upset with dad because *I* am having doubts myself? Do I want my father to give me the okay because *I* lack the confidence to do this on my own?

Many young adult daughters tell me that they feel too guilty or afraid to let their father know what's going on in their private lives: "I don't want him to think less of me." "I couldn't stand to disappoint him." "I don't want to upset him." "He's too religious and conservative to handle this." If you feel this way, you end up lying and hiding the most important things about your personal life from your father. At the same time, though, you don't feel so good about lying and intentionally deceiving him, do you? So how long are you going to let the lies and deception go on? What I'm getting at is this: At some point you have to give yourself permission to make your own decisions without being guilty or afraid of your father's disapproval. At some point you have to ask yourself: At what age are my decisions about sex and my personal lifestyle not going to be affected by what my father thinks? At what age am I going to let my own values—not my father's—determine what I do or do not feel guilty about or ashamed of?

Let me give you a few typical examples. If your father disapproves of premarital sex, are you going to feel guilty because you're not a virgin at age 30 even though you've never been married—how about at age 20? Are you still going to pretend with your dad that you've never had sex when you're 30—how about 20? Or if you've decided to marry a man of a different faith and your father says that you're breaking his heart and he's not coming to your wedding, are you going to let him affect your decision? If you've decided to live with your boyfriend while you're still in college, are you going to hide this from your father because he is still giving you money for school? What about when your dad isn't giving you any money anymore? Then will you feel more comfortable letting him know about your lifestyle choices? I can't answer these questions for you. In fact, there are no correct answers because we all have different values and beliefs about these things. What I am saying, though, is that at some point you need to get rid of the guilt, the fear, the deception, and the lies that come from being so dependent on what your father thinks of your sexual and lifestyle choices.

Handling Your Differences

Regardless of how old you are, you and your father probably will disagree over some things when it comes to sex, dating, marriage, and lifestyles. So when you do have a difference of opinion, what can you do? How are you supposed to let your father know who you are and what you believe when you know he's going to disagree or disapprove? How do you keep the decisions you've made in your personal life from damaging your father-daughter relationship? How can you be yourself around your father when you know that he doesn't—or wouldn't—approve of what you're doing? I offer you eight pieces of advice that have helped most of the daughters with whom I work.

1. *Do not to try to change your father's opinions.* I'm not saying that you shouldn't let your father know why you believe what you do—just like he might share facts or experiences that have lead him to his opinions. But your goal should not be to change his mind, to get him to agree with you, or to get him to approve of what you're doing. Unfortunately, we often start out with exactly this goal: to win dad over to our way of seeing things and to get him to vote "yes" on whatever decision we've made or opinion we have. So we launch in, giving him example after example, fact after fact, story after story. And then he responds with his own examples, facts, and stories. The problem with this approach is that it rarely works. The harder we try to get the other person to agree with us, the more we both dig in and cling to our opinions. If either of you ever does change your opinion, it usually happens gradually and as a result of some quiet, private process—not because of a sudden awakening or a persuasive discussion. You also end up frustrated because you never seem to win these arguments with your dad. And that makes you feel bad because you think that it means he doesn't respect your opinions. You're also mad at yourself because you couldn't think of the right things to say, couldn't think quickly enough, or got too emotional to express yourself rationally and intelligently. What's really happening is that neither you nor your dad is going to change your mind about very personal lifestyle issues. If you had realized this at the beginning, you probably could have explained your opinions or your decisions to him more rationally and more calmly. But because you are so intent on changing him or getting his approval, you express yourself poorly, and you take his remarks as personal

insults. Again, you're better off if your only goal is to let your father know who you are and what you believe—not to win him over to anything. If either you or your father changes your mind and ends up with the same belief, it's probably going to happen through a gradual, silent process, not because of a sudden awakening or a persuasive argument.

2 *Be more compassionate.* Remember that your father, just like you, has opinions that come from what he has been *taught* and from his experiences. Your father didn't pop into the world with any beliefs or opinions about sex or relationships. His beliefs were learned, just like yours. And what he happened to be taught wasn't something he had much control over.

3. *Consider your father's motives.* Some of his feelings and beliefs may have less to do with sex than with worries about your financial or social well-being. Let's go back—way, way back. Where did fathers' beliefs or feelings about their daughters' virginity come from? Why were fathers concerned about their daughters being virgins when they married? In biblical times, why was a man punished more severely for raping an unmarried woman than for raping a married woman? The answer is pretty simple: money. If a daughter was not a virgin— either because she was raped or because she decided to have sex before marriage—most men would never marry her. And if she was not a virgin, her father had to provide a larger dowry (money, animals, household furnishings, land, and so on) to any man who would agree to marry her. If she became pregnant, there would be no husband to provide for her or the child. The financial burden fell on her father and, after his death, on her oldest brother. Her father and brothers literally paid a price for her not being a virgin. So a daughter's virginity was of great concern—not for religious or moral reasons, but for financial ones. Even in our own country, until recent decades, the daughter and father often paid a price if she wasn't a virgin when time came to marry—especially if she had a child. Fewer men were willing to marry a woman with a "bad reputation"—a woman who wasn't a virgin. With her spoiled reputation, the daughter had less chance of "marrying well." And if no man ever married her, she

might end up financially dependent on her father until he died. Even as recently as your grandfather's generation, daughters who were not virgins when they married were looked down on. Again, many fathers were less concerned about "sin" than about the financial and emotional price their daughter would have to pay for not being a virgin. As outdated or offensive as this may seem, even today there are men who don't want to marry a woman who has had "too many" lovers or "too much" sexual experience—certainly not more experience than her husband has had. And some men still want to marry virgins even though they themselves are not. In short, fathers historically have been trying to protect their daughters from ending up being scorned, outcast, and financially ruined.[8]

4. *Reassure your father.* Let your father know that you haven't made your decision with your eyes closed like a little child. Reassure him that you are aware of the problems you're probably going to face because of certain decisions you've made in your personal life. For example, if you're dating someone of another race, reassure your father that you know that you may encounter a certain amount of prejudice and hostility. Or if you're gay and have decided to adopt a child, reassure your father that you have studied the research enough to know that children raised by gay parents are just as well adjusted as kids raised by heterosexual parents.

5. *Watch movies together or read stories written by fathers and by daughters that deal with the issues that create tension between you.* If you can't actually sit down together to watch the films together, then ask your dad to watch them on his own and discuss them with you later. You can do this by phone or even in a letter if that makes you more comfortable. As we've discussed in earlier chapters, watching movies and discussing them can help you to solve certain problems and start talking about difficult issues. The movies and books I've listed for you in the following box are about fathers and adult children dealing with issues such as premarital sex, living with someone before marriage, interracial dating, gay relationships, and pregnancy outside of marriage.

Films and Stories: Sex and Romance

Sex, Dating, and Marriage

Father of the Bride

Meet the Parents

Betsy's Wedding

A Soldier's Daughter Never Cries

Snapper

About Schmidt

Interracial/Intercultural Relationships

My Big Fat Greek Wedding

Jungle Fever

Mississippi Marsala

Fiddler on the Roof

Guess Who's Coming to Dinner?

Gay and Lesbian Issues

Oranges Are Not the Only Fruit

The Wedding Banquet

Torch Song Trilogy

Books: Fiction and Essays

My Father Dancing: Stories [9]

Fathers: Reflections by Daughters [10]

Fathers and Daughters: Stories by Best Selling Authors [11]

Fathers and Daughters: Portraits in Fiction [12]

6. *Do not use emotional blackmail.* Don't allow your father to blackmail you emotionally—and don't blackmail him. As you may remember from Chapter 3, when someone is trying to blackmail you emotionally into doing what they want, they use fear, obligation, and guilt (FOG). As an adult, you cannot allow your father to blackmail

you into doing what he wants in your personal or sexual life by making you afraid that he's going to stop loving you, making you feel obligated to him for all he's done for you, or making you feel guilty for your beliefs and decisions. Remembering what we've already discussed, you might say such things as this when he disapproves of your choices: "I feel bad that you're upset with me; but I'm still going to live with my boyfriend." "I can understand why you believe what you do, but I'm not going to agree to stop dating Joe just because he's not a member of our culture." "That's an interesting point, and I understand very clearly what you believe, but I've already made my decision to go ahead and get married this summer." "Dad, up to now I've been so afraid of disappointing you that I've always said yes to what you wanted. But I'm not going to agree to do things anymore that I truly believe are bad for me—like breaking up with my boyfriend." "I figured you wouldn't be happy with my decision given your religious beliefs, but I am gay and I am not going to lie about that part of who I am." "I'm sorry that you don't want to come to my wedding because you disapprove of this, but I guess that's the way it's going to be because I'm not calling off the marriage." "Neither of us is a bad or immoral person; we just have different principles. So we'll just have to accept the fact that we're not clones of each other." Or "I know you're hurt, but I can't do something that I don't believe in just to make you happy, and this decision isn't something I can compromise on."

7. *Let your father know that you want his acceptance, not his approval.* Also let him know that you *accept* him even though you do not *approve* of his opinions. Acceptance and approval are not the same. *Accepting* someone means that even though we don't agree with some of the choices they have made or some of their beliefs, we continue to love them and to treat them with respect. We don't try to make the person feel guilty or ashamed of his or her choices or his or her beliefs. We don't allow our different opinions to damage our relationship. On the other hand, we don't have to lie or to pretend to *approve of* each other's choices or beliefs. By letting your dad know

that you don't expect him to change his beliefs or give up being who he is, you take the pressure off him. By letting him know that all you want is for him to accept and love you even though you aren't his clone, you reassure him that he does not have to abandon his principles or his beliefs. Once you're an adult, neither you nor your parent should try to impose your beliefs on each other or feel guilty or angry when you can't get the other to approve of your decisions. When we love each other, we don't punish, pressure, or condemn each other for our different beliefs and choices. We accept each other without having to approve.

Don't misunderstand me. I'm not saying that you or your father should respect or accept one another's beliefs or decisions on all matters. And I'm not saying that there may not be situations where a father or daughter ends their relationship as a result of certain things that one of them has done. There are beliefs and actions that are immoral and intolerable under any circumstances. These beliefs and actions do and should have a negative impact on our relationships. In the sexual or social realm, these unacceptable actions include such things as physically abusing another person, having sex with children, raping someone, and attacking people physically because you don't approve of their lifestyle. When I'm saying that you and your father need to *accept* one another despite your differences, I'm not referring to acts such as these that mentally well people throughout the world have always agreed are immoral, unethical, or criminal.

Let's consider one fairly common situation. Assume that your father disapproves of your living with your boyfriend. And he certainly doesn't feel comfortable with the idea of you and your lover sleeping together in his home when you come to visit. As an adult, you shouldn't hide or lie about this important part of your life. Yet you also shouldn't demand or expect your dad to give up his beliefs or to pretend to approve of your lifestyle. No, he shouldn't try to punish you by saying you can't bring your boyfriend home for the holidays or by lecturing the two of you about your lifestyle. But yes, he has the right to tell you how he feels without your withdrawing, lecturing, insulting, or getting angry at him. And yes, he has the right to say that if you and your boyfriend want to spend the night in his home, you won't make a fuss about sleeping in separate rooms. On the other hand, your dad should not punish you in any way if you and your lover decide to stay in a motel whenever you visit him. And your dad certainly shouldn't expect you and your lover to sleep in separate rooms if he chooses to spend the night at your house.

Anyway, not only should your father not try to force his sexual beliefs onto you, you also shouldn't try to force yours onto him. Let me tell you about Suzanne. After her parents divorced, she found out that their marriage had ended because her father was gay. Even though she was a teenager, she wasn't embarrassed by or angry at her father. As a college senior, she explained it this way to me: "I knew my dad was a great parent, and that's all the mattered to me. I wouldn't have wanted him or my mom to lie to me." On the other hand, another daughter, Luanne, told me that she had suspected for the past 14 years since her parents' divorce that her father was gay. Luanne was living with her boyfriend—a man of a different race. Even though her father had told her he didn't approve of her arrangement, he had agreed to allow her boyfriend to join the family in her college graduation festivities. Yet, when her father finally told her that he was gay, both she and her sister turned against him. "It's just so disgusting. I mean, he actually wanted me to meet his male 'friend'." Somehow she had convinced herself that because he was a father, he should accept her lifestyle without expecting her to accept his.

8. *Try to keep yourself and your father focused on your relationship, not on the particular beliefs over which you disagree.* It's been said: "What we choose to focus on enlarges." So if we choose to focus on whatever differences we have, we create and enlarge the gap between us. But if we choose instead to focus on what brings us joy in our father-daughter relationship, we enlarge our love and appreciation for one another. If either you or your father focuses too much on what you each believe or do in your sexual, romantic lives, your relationship is bound to suffer. I've seen too many a daughter reject or punish her

father emotionally because he made choices that she disapproved of: He marries a woman she doesn't like. He decides to let people know that he is gay. He fathers another child late in life. And I've seen too many a daughter rejected or punished emotionally by her father for her choices: She is dating a man he dislikes. She is living with her boyfriend. She has a child outside of marriage. My hope is that you and your father can be loving, wise, and mature enough to allow each other to live according to your own principles and preferences—to focus on what you love about your father-daughter relationship rather than on issues that could divide you.

Chapter 7

Divorce and Remarriage
Resolving, Renewing, Repairing

- Did your parents' divorce damage your relationship with your father?

- Have you blamed him for problems in your life since the divorce?

- Has your relationship been more difficult since he remarried?

- Are there things you would like to ask him about the divorce but haven't?

- Have you been jealous or resentful of his other children?

Like most daughters with divorced parents, you probably answered yes to at least one of these questions. Although it may not be much comfort to you, only 20 percent of the daughters in our country have parents who get married and stay married.[1] The good news is that most daughters do not develop serious, long-term, ongoing problems as a result of their parents' divorce. This doesn't mean that the divorce has no impact at all. Everyone in the family undergoes tremendous upheaval. Still, your parents' divorce is not likely to leave you permanently scarred with serious, long-lasting problems. On the other hand, one area of your life is almost always negatively affected—your relationship with your father. The damage can be relatively minor and short-lived or devastating and permanent. In the worst case, you and your dad may loose your relationship altogether. The greater the damage to your father-daughter relationship, the more likely you are to have ongoing problems—difficulty trusting, being intimate, or maintaining long-term relationships with men; lower achievement in school and at work; depression and eating disorders; and less self-confidence.[2-5]

151

In this chapter we'll be focusing on the situations, beliefs, and behaviors that generally do the most damage to your father-daughter relationship. By understanding what went wrong, you have more power now to renew your relationship and to resolve those issues which still trouble you. Even though they may have divorced years ago, you still may feel hurt or angry because you think that your parents should have stayed married for the sake of you kids. If this is how you feel, focus on this reality: More long-term damage is done to children who live with unhappily married parents than to children whose parents get divorced. Those children who do have serious, ongoing problems after their parents' divorce generally began having those problems while their parents were still married.[2-6] It's the unhappy marriage, not the divorce, that does the most damage. If you insist on holding your parents' responsible for whatever problems you've had since they separated, you'll have to blame them for being unhappily married while they were raising you—not for getting divorced.

Before going further, use this first quiz to think back to how you saw your parents in the first year or so after they stopped living together. We'll come back to this quiz later.

Good Guys and Bad Guys

How did you see your parents after their divorce?

12 Negatives

Mom Dad

___ ___ Sad/depressed

___ ___ Tense/anxious

___ ___ Needy/dependent

___ ___ Illogical/irrational

___ ___ Angry/vengeful

___ ___ Critical/judgmental

___ ___ Deceptive/manipulative

____ ____ Dishonest/untrustworthy

____ ____ Self-pitying/pessimistic

____ ____ Guilt-ridden/ashamed

____ ____ Selfish/self-absorbed

____ ____ Materialistic/greedy

____ ____ Scores

12 Positives

Mom Dad

____ ____ Introspective/reflective

____ ____ Forgiving

____ ____ Nurturing/comforting

____ ____ Loving/kind

____ ____ Generous/fair

____ ____ Sympathetic/understanding

____ ____ Reliable/trustworthy

____ ____ Upbeat/hopeful

____ ____ Satisfied/fulfilled

____ ____ Wise/helpful

____ ____ Caring/concerned

____ ____ Honest/straightforward

____ ____ Scores

Demoralizing, Demeaning, and Dumping Divorced Dads

After your parents divorced, did you feel that your father spent too little time with you or gradually withdrew from your life? The reality is that a large number of fathers do spend less time with their children as the time passes. Yet these same fathers usually say that they wanted to be more involved with their kids. Then why did they seem to lose interest, to pull away, or in some cases to disappear altogether from their children's lives? As for you, if your father did withdraw or seemed less and less interested in your life, why? When you were younger, you probably felt that there was a very simple answer to this question: Because dad doesn't love me anymore. But now that you're older, it's time to look more closely at your father's situation. What was he up against at the time of the divorce?

Let's travel back in time to your parents' divorce. For now, put aside how you felt, and imagine yourself in your father's place. If your dad is like the majority of divorced men, here's what happened to him: He no longer had any say in making decisions about some of the most important things in your life—your education, medical care, or religious upbringing—because only 1 in 10 fathers has joint custody.[7] Without joint custody, he had no way to stop your mother from moving you to another state if that's what she decided to do. If he went to a lawyer to talk about getting joint custody, he probably was told not to bother because judges tend to rule in favor of mothers and because custody battles are costly, time-consuming, and painful for everyone. So your dad probably was denied the right to see you except on alternate weekends, on certain holidays, and perhaps one evening midweek. Obviously this schedule only works well if he lives close enough to your mother and if your school schedule and his work schedule make it possible for you to spend these little pockets of time together. If he was one of the 40 percent of fathers who don't live in the same state with their children (usually because their jobs force them to move or because the mother has moved the kids with her to another state), your time together was even more restricted. In a sense, the legal system fired your dad as your parent while allowing your mom to remain a full-fledged parent.[8] By the way, in the few states that automatically give the father joint custody and guarantee that his children can live with him for at least one-third of the year, fewer mothers are filing for divorce.[9]

Too many teachers, school counselors, and medical workers also fire fathers from being parents after a divorce.[10–13] Many of these adults ignore the divorced father or treat him like a second-class parent. If this was the case for you, these adults continued to involve and to interact with your mother. But most of them excluded or ignored your father—giving your mother the power to decide how much to share with him about your life. Feeling unwanted and unappreciated, many dads slowly give up hope and withdraw.

Yes, there are fathers who pull away from their children no matter how much encouragement they get to stay involved. Your dad may have been part of this minority—and it is a minority. But before you jump to the conclusion that your father wanted to withdraw from you, consider how the overwhelming majority of dads are pushed out of their children's lives by the legal system and by other adults.

As you think back to how your father behaved, use the following quiz to consider what may have been going on in his life at the time. Better yet, send him the quiz and ask him to talk to you about his experiences. *Warning:* Before you do this, let him know that you don't want to talk about how your mother treated him. At this point, you just want to know how all the other adults in your life treated him—your teachers, counselors, doctors, coaches, and neighbors. Keep the conversation going with questions such as these: Which adults in my life made you feel the most valued as a father after the divorce, and what kinds of things did they do? What did people do that made it harder for you to be involved in my life? What hurt you most in terms of how you got treated as my parent? Do you know other divorced men who felt the way you did? Did you ever talk to anyone about how you felt or how you were being excluded or ignored?

Was Your Dad Dumped as a Parent?

Think back to the years after your parents' divorce. How often did these things happen? How many "I'm not sure" answers do you have? Why not ask your father to take this quiz and let him tell you how he was treated as a parent? In addressing these statements, use ? to mean "I'm not sure," 0 to mean "no/never," 1 to mean "rarely," 2 to mean "fairly often," and 3 to mean "almost always/yes."

____ My father was given joint custody without having to hire a lawyer.

____ My father was legally allowed to have almost as much time with us kids as our mother had.

____ My friends treated my dad the same way they did when my parents were married.

(Continued)

___ My doctors and dentists kept my father informed about me just like they did for my mother.

___ My coaches sent information to my father just like they did for my mother.

___ If I ever saw a therapist, he or she made sure my father was included and felt welcomed.

___ My teachers made sure that my father was invited and welcomed in parent activities.

___ My friends' parents continued to treat my father like a full-fledged parent.

___ My dad was told far enough in advance about my activities so that he could arrange to attend.

___ Adults in our religious community continued to treat my father as a full-fledged parent.

___ Score (30 possible)

Your father also had another powerful force working against his relationship with you: the negative beliefs and inaccurate information so many of us have about divorced fathers. Take a look at the following quiz to see how many negative things you believed at the time your parents stopped living together.

Divorced Dads: What Do You Believe?

At the time of your parents' divorce, what did you believe about divorced men?

___ Most divorces happen because the man falls in love with another woman.

___ Most divorces happen because the husband is abusive, alcoholic, or emotionally unstable.

___ Fathers are far more likely than mothers to commit adultery.

____ Fathers generally lose interest in their children after a divorce.

____ Financially, most fathers come out much better than mothers after divorce.

____ Mothers are usually more depressed than fathers after a divorce.

____ College-educated mothers are generally less angry after a divorce than less educated women.

____ Divorced men usually remarry much younger women.

____ The husband is usually the person who wants the divorce.

____ Most divorced fathers do not make their child support payments.

____ Score (10 possible trues)

How many did you think were true? The correct answer is zero. Not one of these statements is true for the vast majority of people in our country, as you can see from the "Eye Openers" that follow. The higher your score, the more difficult it was for you and your dad to stay bonded because you already had so many negative beliefs and assumptions about divorced men. Imagine how your father must have felt knowing that many people in our society believe these negative things about divorced dads.

Long before your parents divorced, you probably had an image of divorced dads something like this: After cheating on his devoted wife with a much younger woman, the father asks for a divorce. Unlike him, the mother has been a loving spouse and dedicated parent. After all she has sacrificed for the family, her husband has abandoned her. She is sad, lonely, and struggling to make ends meet while dad is having the time of his life—the carefree, swinging bachelor. In fact, dad is having so much fun that he hardly misses his children at all. When he does spend time with them he isn't a very good parent. And he's probably a "deadbeat dad" who has stopped paying child support so that he can spend the money on himself, his girlfriend, or his new family.

Negative messages such as this are easy to find in movies, magazines, and television shows.[14] Generally speaking, stories about divorced parents emphasize mom's strengths and dad's shortcomings. Dad is the powerful

---

Eye Openers

- Women are *more likely* than men to get divorced because they have fallen in love with someone else and are almost as likely as men to commit adultery.[16,17]
- Two-thirds of divorces are initiated by the wife, generally because she doesn't feel that her husband meets her emotional needs or communicates well enough.[18]
- More than 80 percent of divorced fathers pay all their child support—and the majority of those who don't are often unemployed or temporarily out of work.[14,19]
- Men are *more likely* than women to be depressed and suicidal after divorce—mainly because they miss their kids.[20,21]
- Many fathers are not better off financially than mothers after their divorce.[14,24]
- College-educated, white mothers tend to be as angry *or angrier* than other mothers about financial matters after a divorce.[7,27]

---

brute. Mom is the powerless victim. Dad is selfish, untrustworthy, shallow, and greedy. Mom is selfless, loyal, wise, and generous. Think about the lousy fathers in the following movies and the misery they cause their daughters: *An Unmarried Woman, Shoot the Moon, Twice in a Lifetime, Affliction,* and *The First Wives Club* (opening weekend, one-third of all moviegoers went to this movie[15]). Now consider the loving, dedicated, mistreated moms in those same movies. Even if they don't get divorced, dad is usually the one who cheats—a loveless, meaningless fling with a woman we can't help but dislike (*Fatal Attraction* and *Terms of Endearment*). But when mom cheats, it's because she's lonely and falls in love with some "nice" guy (*Bridges of Madison County, The Horse Whisperer,* and *Unfaithful*).

So what's the big deal? The big deal is what we discussed in Chapter 1: The beliefs we have about any group of people influence what we see, what we remember, and how we treat them—even when our beliefs are not based on fact. This means that you were already inclined to see and to assume the worst about your father and the best about your mother. On top of everything else he had to deal with as a newly divorced parent, your father had this working against him as well.

Money—The Never-Ending Battle

Rarely do I meet a daughter with divorced parents who doesn't have some bad feelings about her father related to money. The three complaints I usually hear are: "Dad didn't treat mom fairly." "He was too selfish and should have given us more because he could afford to." "Dad complained too much and was overly sensitive about the money stuff." The following quiz will help you recall how you felt about your dad and money.

Money—How Nice a Guy Is Dad?

In addressing these statements, use 0 to mean "never," 1 to mean "rarely," 2 to mean "about half the time," and 3 to mean "regularly."

____ My father was too stingy and selfish.

____ He didn't treat my mom fairly in terms of money.

____ Dad shouldn't complain about how mom spends his child support money.

____ Dad should pay for our college educations because he makes more money than mom.

____ Dad shouldn't ever say anything about how much of his money is being spent on us.

____ If it weren't for dad, mom would be in a better situation financially.

____ Dad should buy me things instead of telling me to get mom to buy them from his child support money.

____ It's not fair that dad is better off financially than mom.

____ If it weren't for my mother, my father wouldn't be the success he is financially.

____ My father isn't paying all that he is supposed to pay by law.

____ Your score (30 possible)

The higher your score, the more likely it is that you had—or still have—some pretty bad feelings about your father and money. If this is the case, mail your father a copy of this quiz. After a week or two, ask him to talk to you about his answers. If you're reluctant to do this, ask yourself *why* you're not willing to hear his side of things. Are you afraid he's going to say something bad about your mother? And if he did, why would that be so upsetting to you? If your mom has had a chance to share her feelings and her version of the financial facts with you, why shouldn't your dad have the same opportunity? The payoff could be a big one for you: feeling better about your father and putting aside some of your anger. Now let's take a closer look at the three complaints I hear most commonly.

Dad Mistreated Mom Financially

Because most parents divorce when their children are young, it's easy for kids to be misled or to become confused over what's going on between their parents financially. And with so many negative beliefs about divorced fathers floating around, regardless of our age, we're prone to assume the worst about dad.

One of our most popular and most damaging assumptions is that fathers are far better off financially than mothers after a divorce. We also may assume that the father is entirely to blame for this unfair situation. This belief took hold almost 20 years ago after a female sociologist wrote a book claiming that a woman's standard of living generally fell by 73 percent and a man's rose by 42 percent after divorce.[22] Her conclusions were cited widely in the media and spread like wildfire. There's only one problem: She was wrong. Nearly 10 years later the author admitted that she had made a mistake, after many researchers had reanalyzed her data and found that, in her small sample of high-income couples, the women's standard of living had fallen by about 25 percent and the men's rose by 10 percent. Even so, this did *not* mean that women's *incoming money* fell by 25 percent or that men's *incomes* rose by 10 percent. The study was referring to *standard of living,* which is *not* the same as income.[14,23]

Trying to figure out how much difference there is between mothers' and fathers' financial situations after a divorce—or who is to blame for any differences that do exist—is no easy matter. Are the statisticians comparing each parent's incoming money *before* or *after* taxes? This matters because as custodial parents whose child support money is tax free, divorced mothers generally have more tax advantages than fathers. Are all the parents' financial assets (house, investments, savings, and cars) being considered or only their cash inflow? Are we talking about the parents' financial situations in the first year of their divorce, when divorced women's incomes are at their lowest, or 2 to 3 years after the divorce, when women's incomes have risen? Are we considering the extra money a father might have to spend beyond child support when his kids are with him? For example, in the largest federally funded study yet conducted, fathers were left with only $25 a month more than mothers after the mother's tax advantages and the father's additional expenses for the kids were considered.[14]

On the whole, mothers generally are worse off than fathers in terms of their incoming money and how many fall below the poverty level after a divorce. However, if we look at both parents' financial situations a year or more after the divorce, the differences grow smaller. And even immediately after divorce, there are mothers who end up better off financially than fathers. The situation also depends on what the mother earned while she was married. If she worked full time throughout her marriage, her financial situation is much more similar to her ex-husband's. But if she was a housewife whose husband earned a high or better-than-average income for the family, then she usually has a greater fall in her standard of living than he does. Because couples with less education and lower incomes are more likely to get divorced and less likely to pay child support than more well-educated parents with higher incomes, poorly educated mothers usually do end up in a much worse situation than the fathers after a divorce.[24,25]

What all this means for your father-daughter relationship is this: Don't jump to conclusions about who was better off financially after the divorce. If you felt that your dad mistreated your mom financially, your relationship with him may benefit from getting more information about their divorce agreement and their financial situations at the time of their divorce. It's possible that one of four situations may have led you to the wrong conclusion. First, men usually remarry before women do. If this was true for you, it means that your father's standard of living improved before your mother's did because he and his wife were living on two incomes, whereas your mom had only one. Although there isn't anything unfair about this, as a child it might have felt unfair to you.

Second, if your mother earned less money than your dad (as 80 percent of married women do), or if she had earned no money (as 20 percent of women do), you may have assumed that your dad was somehow responsible for her not being able to earn as much money as he did.[1] Maybe you believed that he had prevented her from having a career or forced her to give up working full time to stay home with you kids. What you probably didn't realize as a child is that most men earn more money than their wives and ex-wives because men generally work more years and work longer hours than women throughout their lives. So even though your father had to give your mother half of everything they owned when they divorced, over time, he would have more money than her because he had a higher income. If this happened to you, it may have created a situation in which you felt sorry for your mom and blamed your dad for the fact that he eventually ended up with more money than she had.

Third, what your mother received from your father when they divorced may not have been obvious or visible to you as a child—such things as equity in the house, ownership of the car, and half their savings and investments. Given your age at the time, you probably didn't realize that divorce agreements generally give women half of all the assets—including half of the man's retirement fund. This is generally true even if the wife never earned any of the family's money during the marriage.

Fourth, if your father earned a lot more than your mother, divorce law requires him to give up a higher percent of his income to support you kids. There is no legal trick that can get a father out of paying child support altogether or that won't charge him more because he earns the higher income. And if your mother was a housewife and your father earned a good income, he probably was required to pay her a "retraining allowance" for several years after their divorce in addition to the child support money he sent for you. This additional money from your dad was intended to enable your mom to go back to school or to get the additional training she needed to support herself.

Dad Mistreated You Financially

Your relationship with your father also has been affected by how you feel he treated *you* financially. First and foremost, do you believe that he paid all his child support or not? Second, did you have the impression that he was generous or that he was stingy? Many of us believe that most divorced men are "deadbeat dads" who refuse to pay their child support—selfish, irresponsible men who have enough money to support their kids, but who refuse. Yes, it is true that millions of fathers are not making any child support payments. But 80 percent of these fathers have never been married to their children's mother—and they typically have little or no income. [1,19] *As for divorced fathers, almost 80 percent pay all their child support. Those who pay only a part or none of what is due are often unemployed or temporarily out of work. And in the spring of 2000, 60 percent of noncustodial fathers spent additional money on their children for clothes, groceries, and gifts.* [1] Moreover, when the mother allows the father some say in how his money is being spent, he almost always pays all his child support and often spends more than required in the divorce agreement.[14]

What all these statistics mean for you is this: If you believe that your father shirked his financial responsibility to you, please talk to him about it. It's possible that he was one of the 20 percent of divorced men who failed to pay. Then again, it's possible that you don't have all the facts and that you're wrong. If the issue still bothers you, it *is* worth giving your father a chance to present his facts and explain his behavior.

If you went to college, your feelings about your dad are also influenced by what he gave you financially during those years. Because the law does not require married parents to pay for college, it's considered unconstitutional to require divorced parents to pay. On the other hand, laws are designed to guarantee that kids receive the same benefits they would have gotten if their parents had stayed married. And since most married parents do send their kids to college if they can afford it, a number of states now allow divorced parents to hire lawyers and take one another back to court for refusing to pay anything for college. As you may know from your own experience, the issue of paying for your college education often unleashes intense emotions and opens up old wounds: How much should your father pay if you have refused to have much to do with him for years? If dad is going to chip in, how much say should he have in what college you choose? What if he is willing to pay for a state university but not for an expensive private school? What if your mother refuses to pay anything because your dad makes much more money than she does? What if your mother claims that she doesn't have enough money to help you out, but your father claims that she does? If you're still upset with your father over issues such as these, tell him how you feel, and give him a chance to share his feelings and his view of the situation with you. Again, if it's important enough that it still bothers you, then it's important enough to talk about because it is detracting from your relationship.

There also may be some tension between you and your dad if he has remarried and you're wondering how he's going to treat you financially when he dies. We may not like to admit it, but when dad has money to leave behind, his kids, step kids, wife, and ex-wife often do start worrying about who's going to get what. Because we're healthier and living longer than ever, more of us are remarrying late in life. And so more daughters may be wondering: How is dad's wife influencing the decisions he's making in his will? Is dad going to leave more to their kids than to me? If inheritance issues are on your mind, the time probably has come for you to talk to your father about his will. The mere thought of doing this may knot up your stomach, but at some point aging parents and adult children need to talk about inheritance issues so that everyone knows what to expect and how to plan their own financial future. Even when very little money is actually involved, financial issues can still be very damaging to your relationship.[26,27]

Dad Was Overly Sensitive About Money

Most daughters tell me that their fathers have made too big a deal about money stuff ever since the divorce. "He gets uptight when anything comes up about money. He talks too much about how much he has spent on me over the years. He complains that I don't appreciate him enough for what he's given me." Sound familiar? So why might dad have behaved that way? What might he be feeling—and fearing?

First, let's consider this reality: At some point after the divorce, many fathers feel that their teenage and adult children are more concerned about what they get from him financially than what he gives them emotionally.[27-29] Dad feels that his kids spend more time with him, show more interest in him, and seem to love him more when he spends money on them—taking them on vacations, giving them money when they come up short, or paying for their health or car insurance even though they're adults. He feels that his love is being measured and monitored by how much money he hands over—and by how willingly and happily he gives it. The point is not whether divorced fathers are right about their children. The point is that this *is* what millions of fathers feel. Somewhere, somehow, many fathers have gotten the impression that giving money is the way their teenage and adult children want them to express their love.

Knowing how so many divorced fathers feel, you may want to ask yourself: Have I ever done anything that could possibly give my dad the impression that the way I feel about him has anything to do with money? When is the last time I phoned or visited him without mentioning a single thing about my having money troubles of some sort? How often does he end up spending money on me when we're together or after I've talked to him? Do I tend to contact him more often at those times of year when he would be likely to give me a gift—my birthday, graduation, engagement, Christmas, or Hanukkah? Have I ever spent more time with him or acted more enthusiastic around him after he has spent money on me?

As you think about how money has affected your relationship, you may want to follow the lead of the daughter I am about to tell you about. About a year ago I got a phone call from a father whose daughter had taken my course. "Dr. Nielsen," he said, "I don't know what you're doing in that course, but whatever it is, keep doing it! My daughter called me at 1:30 in the morning to thank me for all that I had done for her financially since her mother and I divorced 14 years ago. You know, I've never said anything to her; but all these years it has hurt my feelings that she always assumed that I should be the parent who pays for everything. Her mom makes a good income, but my daughter never asks her for any money. I've always been happy to give her the money, but it really blew me away that she finally thanked me. And it wasn't my birthday or anything."

Mother: Her Opinions and Her Well-Being

Remember from Chapter 5 how much power your mother has had in shaping the kind of relationship you and your father have? Well, when your parents divorce, there's a major *power surge*—your mom's power increases far beyond what it was during their marriage. Because almost all children spend far more time with mother than with father after a divorce, mom has the stage pretty much to herself. On that stage she holds the microphone. And with that microphone she lets you know how she feels about your father and about the divorce. Even though she may never say anything directly to you about your dad, she gets her feelings and her opinions across in other ways—the expressions on her face, her tone of voice, the way she acts after she's talked to him, the way she looks and acts before you go to your dad's, and her "joking" comments or the remarks she makes about "some people I know"—meaning your father. A mother might say, "I want you to have a good relationship with your dad and don't blame him for the divorce." Yet at the same time she can send a different message with the look on her face or her tone of voice: "Your dad's the jerk who broke up our family, and I don't think he's nearly as good a parent as I am."

Hopefully, your mom created a positive image of your father. Millions of children, however, get a negative impression from their mother—especially if dad remarries and mom is still single. Millions of fathers feel that their ex-wives are undermining their relationships with the children. Those fathers who eventually withdraw from their kids often say that they felt that their children were losing interest or being turned against them by their mother. Feeling powerless, unwanted, and heart-broken, the father gradually backs away. In other words, the more your mother convinces *you and your father* that she wholeheartedly and enthusiastically wants you to have a loving, involved relationship, the more likely it is to happen. [28-30]

Aside from the impressions your mother gives you of your father, how well she adapts to the divorce has a huge impact on your relationship with him. Now look back at your answers on the checklist at the beginning of this chapter. How did you see each of your parents after the divorce? If you checked almost as many positives and negatives for each of your parents, that's good news for your father-daughter relationship. It means that you didn't see your mother as the "good guy" and your father as the "bad guy." Above all, it's important that you saw your mother and your father adapting equally well to the divorce as time passed. As you can see from the next set of "Eye Openers," though, most daughters do end up seeing dad as the bad guy and believing that he's adapting much better than mom. The next quiz can help you to focus more closely on how well you felt your parents were adapting and moving forward with their lives.

How Are Mom and Dad Doing?

How did you think each of your parents were doing in the first year or two after their divorce? In addressing these statements, use 0 to mean "never," 1 to mean "rarely," 2 to mean "quite a bit," and 3 to mean "almost always."

Mom Dad

____ ____ I'm relatively happy with my life even though the divorce was painful.

____ ____ I can take care of myself emotionally and financially without help from you kids.

____ ____ You don't need to worry about me.

____ ____ There's no reason for you to pity me or feel sorry for me.

____ ____ I am responsible for making myself happy.

____ ____ I have adult friends who can help me solve my problems.

____ ____ Of course I'm upset by the divorce, but I'm going to be fine.

____ ____ I'm enjoying myself with friends and activities other than you kids.

____ ____ When I'm talking to my friends, it's mainly about happy things.

____ ____ I'm hoping to get married again some day.

____ ____ Score (30 possible)

The higher the scores you gave your mom, the more likely it is that your relationship with your father survived the divorce in pretty good shape. You felt that your mother was doing a pretty good job taking care of herself—emotionally, physically, socially, and financially. Seeing that she was getting back on her feet and adjusting to her new life, you weren't as likely to feel disloyal or guilty about spending time with your father. You felt free to fully enjoy your relationship with him. And because you didn't feel that you had to take care of your mother emotionally, you didn't become her counselor or her best friend. You weren't having to help her work through any angry or hurt feelings she may have been having about your father. The lower your mother's score, the more your relationship with your father was damaged by the divorce. Feeling that your mother wasn't adjusting well to her new life, you got too focused on making her happy and helping her resolve her problems. You also tended to blame your dad for your mom's troubles. You even may have felt that your being with him made your mother even more unhappy.

If you gave your mom a low score and your dad a high score, your father-daughter relationship suffered a lot after their divorce. You believed that your mom wasn't doing well and that your dad seemed to be doing just fine. You became her protector and her defender. If you felt sorry for

Eye Openers

- After a divorce, nonwhite mothers and mothers who have always been employed full time are generally the most supportive of the father's relationship with their children.[30,31]
- The parent who feels guiltiest about the divorce tends to adjust more slowly afterwards and to give the kids too much power.[32,33]
- A divorced mother who grew up with a loving relationship with her own parents tends to be more supportive of her ex-husband's relationship with their children.[34–36]
- A college-educated mother is *not* necessarily more supportive of her ex-husband's relationship with their children than a less well educated mother.[27-33]

your mother but not for your father, you tended to see the divorce from her viewpoint and to see him as unhurt and invincible. If your mother allowed or encouraged you to feel sorry for her or to see her as powerless or fragile, she was wielding tremendous power over your relationship with your father—a power that you, as a child, were not mature enough to recognize. Acting like a victim or getting people to feel sorry for us is one of the most manipulative and powerful ways to control other people—especially children, because they aren't aware of what we're doing to them.

Dad Remarries

When you think about a divorced dad getting remarried, what pops into your head? According to most fairy tales, movies, and TV programs, here's what you were programmed to expect and to believe about your dad: [37-39] Your dad is such a blockhead that he has married way too soon and has chosen a woman who is bad news for you and your mother. Either she's a sexy young airhead, a greedy mooch who's after his money, a self-centered career woman who hates kids, a jealous shrew who doesn't want your dad to have a close relationship with you, or a tyrant who transforms him into a bumbling fool and a terrible parent. Your father and his wife are nowhere near as trustworthy, loving, sensitive, unselfish, or well-intentioned as your mother. When it comes right down to it, you've got a lot in common with Hansel and Gretel, whose dad allows his new wife to send his kids into the woods where a witch tries to burn them alive in the oven of her gingerbread house, and Snow White, whose dad allowed his vain, jealous wife to put his daughter into a coma with a poison apple. In short, you better be sad and on guard because your father's marriage is bad news for you.

If your situation is like the vast majority's, here is what usually happens when your father remarries.[40-44] To begin with, your father and his wife have the disadvantage of being first to change the life you have gotten used to while your parents were both still single. Roughly 80 percent of men remarry within 3 years, and 80 percent of their ex-wives remarry within 5 years. So your dad and his wife have to bear the brunt of your adjusting to a parent getting remarried. Especially during the first few years, it seems as if someone (or everyone) is jealous, angry, insecure, sad, suspicious, or upset. These feelings and conflicts may get so intense that you and your dad are literally pulled apart—maybe for weeks, maybe for years. If your dad and his new wife have children together, or if she already has children of her own, things are usually more strained between you and your dad. For the first few years (maybe still?) somebody gets tense or hurt whenever your parents or their spouses have to be around each other—graduations, weddings, holidays, and funerals. How your relationship with your father eventually ends up generally depends on four things: your mom's feelings, your feelings about your dad's other kids, dad and his wife's expectations, and the way you treat his wife.

Mother's Feelings and Circumstances

There's a saying: "When mama ain't happy, ain't *nobody* happy!" When your dad remarried, how happy was your mother with her own life and with his remarrying? Hopefully, you didn't have to find out firsthand that your relationship with your father (and his wife) is generally at its worst when "mama ain't happy." It's best for your father-daughter relationship when you and your mother feel that she has *as much* in her life as your dad has in his—as much joy, money, serenity, laughter, romance, vitality, and hope for a happy future. This is why your relationship with your dad almost always improves after your mom remarries. Until then, you may have encountered what these daughters did: "Mom was always reminding me in one way or another that dad was more cooperative and flexible before he remarried. That made me resent him and his wife. Looking back on it now, maybe he just quit letting mom treat him like he and she were still married to each other." "Dad and his wife both had very successful careers and good incomes. Mom often pointed out that she wasn't 'the *kind* of person' who needed a lot of money or a prestigious job. It was as if she wanted me to think that dad and his wife were self-centered and shallow and that she was the wise one who lived this 'meaningful' life." "Even though mother said, 'Have a nice time, sweetie,' whenever I went to see my dad and his wife, she'd look really sad, and in her softest voice she'd tell me how much she was going to miss me. I'd feel guilty and end up phoning her while I was at his place, just to be sure that she was okay. Even now when I go home to visit, I feel that I have to go to my mother's before I go to my dad's." "My mother exploded when the school listed my stepmother as one of the people to contact in case of emergencies. She always seemed jealous or hurt when my dad's wife was involved in any important way in my life." For better or for worse, your mother's feelings and her circumstances shape your relationship with your dad and his wife.

Dad's Other Kids

Have you ever been jealous or resentful of your father's other children? Have you ever felt that he gave them more or loved them more than you—or that they had replaced you altogether? If so, your relationship with your father certainly suffered somewhere along the line. If you still feel this way at times, what can you do at this point? If you have children yourself, you already know that kids are not interchangeable objects. You have a unique and different kind of relationship with each of your children. If you don't have kids yet, you may not understand that a parent can't just substitute or replace one kid for another. You may need to keep reminding yourself: Just because my father loves another child does *not* mean that he loves me any less. Your father's love is not like a chocolate pie with a limited number of pieces to be handed out—one piece for each of his other children, one piece for his new wife, and then, Oops! No piece left for you. Your father knows that he has enough love for all of you—but do you?

If you feel that your father pays less attention to you than to his other kids, have you told him? Are you just silently steaming and pouting—blaming him because he ought to know how you feel? Yes? Then it's time to tell him how you feel. Even if you are a lot older than his other kids, you are *not* being childish by telling him that you'd like more attention from him. What *is* childish is to hide your feelings and deny him the chance to make you feel better by giving you what you want from him. Remember from Chapter 3: You have to ask for what you want in the right way. Don't make mean-spirited or snide remarks about his other kids. Don't talk to him when you're upset over something that has just happened between you. Talk when you're calm. Talk when you're alone. Talk when he's not preoccupied or rushed. Most important, *be specific* about what you want—more time alone with him, more phone calls, more compliments, or more money? Don't make vague statements such as "I need more attention" or "I need you to make me feel that you love me as much as you love my half-sister." A clear request may sound like this: "Dad, I know this might sound a little silly to you, but I'd really like to have more time alone with you. I love you, and I'd like the two of us to spend a few hours off by ourselves whenever I come to visit. I'm happy to spend time with your wife and the other kids. It's just that I'd like us to be able to focus more on each other, and that's hard to do with other people around. How would you feel about the two of us going for a long hike or going out for a leisurely meal every time I'm here?"

Do you think your father is a better parent to his new kids than he was to you? If you are right, hurrah for him! I hope that he *is* a better father now than he was in the past. Wouldn't it be great if all adults learned to be better parents than they were when they were younger? The real question is: *Why* wouldn't you want your father to change for the better as he ages? If he were making the same mistakes that you think he made with you, *why* would that make you happy? *What is it that is really bothering you?* Is it possible that you've been wrong about him all this time—possible that he is more loving and more willing to change than you always imagined? Or are you angry and jealous because you want what he's giving his other kids. Do you feel like saying, "Damn it, dad! Finally, you're the father I always wanted. But it's too late for me to benefit from the new, improved you. That's not fair!"

If this is how you feel, there's good news: You *can* have your share of the new, improved dad. What's stopping you from reaching out for what he now has to offer you? If he's less focused on work and more focused on family nowadays, then spend more time with him. If he's not as tense or uptight as he was as a young father, good for you—enjoy it. Stop looking back into the past. Stop blaming him because he has matured and improved. *Embrace the father he has become.*

Dad and His Wife's Expectations

A third reason why your relationship with your dad might be damaged when he remarries is because he or his wife have such unrealistic ideas about what the three of you are supposed to become—a "blended" or "step" family. Yes, the three of you should strive to become in many ways like a family *if you live with your father and his wife while you are growing.* By *live with,* I mean more than weekend visits. I mean living in their home on a regular basis throughout the school year. If you're like 90 percent of the children in our country, you have never lived on a daily basis with your dad and his wife because your time with him was legally restricted to weekends or holidays— or because your father remarried after you had already left home. So here's the dilemma: We're bombarded with the message that the best and the most loving people become just like a family to each other when dad or mom remarries. You and your dad's wife eventually are supposed to be like mother and daughter—not like aunt and niece, not like friends, and not like friendly social acquaintances. This expectation, this desire, this belief, creates a heap of tension for your father-daughter relationship—and for your father's marriage as well. Frankly, I wish we could eliminate the word *step* from our remarried-family vocabulary. The word itself supports the goofy idea that a daughter has to become friends with or has to love her father's wife if she truly loves her father and wants to make him happy— and the goofy idea that a father's marriage is better if his child and his wife form some special bond.

If the three of you don't achieve this "family thing" (which the vast majority of us don't), then one or all of you feel that you have failed some-how. Your dad may feel that he has failed his wife or failed you because he couldn't get you and her to do that buddy-buddy or mother-daughter thing. Or his wife may feel that she's failed your dad or failed you, just as you feel that you've failed your dad because this bonding isn't happening between you and her. In the meantime, your mom is probably climbing the walls or wringing her hands worrying about all the bonding that is supposed to be going on between you and your dad's wife. No wonder everyone is uptight.

So now what? First, all three of you would benefit if you talk about what's going on. Your father-daughter relationship and their marriage is placed under unnecessary strain when you feel that your dad is pushing his wife at you—or urging you to make him happy by spending more time with her. If you're too uncomfortable to talk with both of them about this, then have a private talk or write a letter to your dad. Say something along these lines: "Dad, because I love you, it makes me feel good to see how happy Rita makes you. I really do appreciate her for the happiness she brings you. Often, though, I feel that you're disappointed or angry at me because she and I aren't close friends. It might be my imagination, but I feel that you're pushing her at me. Because I don't get to spend as much time as I'd like with you, I really want time alone with you. When I get married, I plan to spend time with you without my husband around. If you and he eventually get to be friends, that's fine. But it's not something I'm going to push at you or at him. Would you be willing to spend time alone with me each time I visit, or would you be willing to make some visits to me without Rita coming along every time?" Let me reassure you: *Every* daughter who has followed my advice and who has worded her request in this way has ended up with more time alone and a more relaxed relationship with her dad.

How You Treat His Wife

You also can boost your relationship with your dad by treating his wife in a friendlier way. Relax! I am *not* saying you and she have to become friends. There's a big difference between being friendlier and being friends. If you think about the people you are friendly to but have no intention of becoming friends with, you know exactly what I mean. The following "evil" stepdaughter quiz can give you ideas for ways to be friendlier to your dad's wife. (How does it feel to be referred to as evil, even jokingly?)

Are You an "Evil" Stepdaughter?

In addressing these statements, use 0 to mean "never," 1 to mean "rarely," 2 to mean "fairly often," and 3 to mean "almost always."

You Dad

___ ___ Thanked his wife for something that she's done for me (other than a gift)

___ ___ Told his wife that I appreciate how happy she makes my dad

___ ___ Apologized for something I've said or done to her

___ ___ Shown an interest in her childhood, family, and friends

___ ___ Asked questions about what's going on in her life

___ ___ Done something nice for one of her children

___ ___ Remembered her birthday without prompting

___ ___ Sent her something from the paper or a magazine that might interest her

___ ___ Told her that I know it must be stressful at times being in her situation

___ ___ Complimented her on something that I know she is proud of

___ ___ Asked her to show me how to do something she does well

___ ___ Said something nice to her about a child or relative of hers

___ ___ Asked for her opinion or advice

___ ___ Included her in pictures we're taking instead of her being the photographer

___ ___ Spent a few minutes talking to her on the phone before asking to speak to dad

___ ___ Scores (45 possible)

The higher your score, the more your relationship with your father benefits. Remember, by being friendly to her, *you* get the payoff—a more relaxed, joyful relationship with your father.

Finally, grant your father the same freedom you want him to grant you—the freedom to have the kind of romantic relationship you want with the person who makes you happy without judgment from your family. Maybe you don't want the kind of marriage your dad has. Maybe you wish that he'd picked a different kind of woman. Maybe you don't like the way they act around each other. Sound familiar? Then ask yourself: What gives me the right to sit in judgment of my father—or to make mean-spirited remarks or jokes about his marriage to other family members? How do I feel (or how would I feel) when he judges or makes fun of the person I am in love with behind my back? What gives either of us the right to judge the other for what makes us happy in the most intimate relationship of our lives? Yes, he is your father. But he is also a *man*—a man who has a private, romantic life—a part of his life that shouldn't be scrutinized or disapproved of by you.

As time passes, you may realize that you made a few mistakes along the way that made your relationship with your dad more difficult after he remarried. So how about apologizing? You'd be amazed what this can do for your relationship. One of the most mature and kindest things I've known a daughter to do is what Annette did after looking at pictures of her father's wedding from many years ago: "When I saw the picture of his and my stepmother's wedding, I almost cried because I vividly remembered sitting there refusing to accept what was happening. I behaved so badly that day. The picture jolted me right back to sitting pinned to a bench, helpless to prevent upheaval once again. I phoned my father and told him how bad I felt about how I had behaved that day. I went on to apologize for some of the things I did in those years after they married. A few days ago, I called my step mom. We talked almost an hour—unprecedented in our relationship after 11 years. I apologized to her for many of the things she had to go through because of me."

Eye Openers

- Getting remarried generally has little impact on how much time a father spends with his children or how much child support money he sends their mother.[43]
- Rarely does a remarried father love or bond with his wife's children as if they were his own.[21,44]
- Being a stepmother is usually far more stressful and more difficult than being a stepfather.[42-46]

Let's end with the worst-case scenario: Your relationship with your father continues to be damaged because you don't want to spend time around him on account of his wife. You've tried your best to be friendly to her, but you and she just don't mix. If things have gotten to this point, you need to tell your dad that for the time being you want to spend all your time with him alone. Don't launch into an attack on his wife. Don't get into the reasons you don't like her. Just say or write something like this: "Dad, Rita and I are so different and I have so much stuff I'm trying to work through right now that it's just not comfortable for me to be with her. I'd even bet she feels the same way I do. For the sake of my relationship with you, for the next few months I need to spend time just with you. Maybe on down the road I'll feel more comfortable around Rita, and the three of us can spend some time together. In the meantime, let's just spend the time we have together with each other."

The Blame Game: Adultery and Other Matters

In your parents' marriage or divorce, who did you see as the "bad guy"? For the sake of your father-daughter relationship, I hope that your answer is "neither." However, if you're like most children, at least for some period of time you sided with your mom against your dad. And this made your relationship with him more distant and more difficult.[28-30]

In part you sided with your mom because you lived with her and because you were more accustomed to talking about personal things with her than with your dad. You were far more likely to hear her versions of the marriage and the divorce than your dad's. You also were inclined to see their marriage and their divorce from her point of view because mothers are much more likely than fathers to lean too much on their kids—especially their daughters—for solace, advice, and emotional support after a divorce. Then, too, as we've already discussed, we're all bombarded with stories about "bad" dads. So we're inclined to assume the worst about divorced men.

Now that you're older, you're probably realizing that you'll never know the complete or unbiased truth about what went on between your parents during their marriage or after their divorce. Your memories and the stories that other people have told you are always biased to some degree—and in some cases they may be completely untrue. So you can't rely only on your memories to give you an accurate picture of what happened. More important, it's very easy to jump to the wrong conclusions about which of your parents was wronged or abandoned, especially if you were young when they separated.

Consider this situation: After your parents' divorce, your dad starts dating different women, but your mom doesn't appear to be seeing anyone. Eventually, mom introduces you to her male "friend." After many months she tells you that he's become more than just a friend. But several years later their relationship ends. In the meantime, your dad has been dating different women and eventually remarries. This really upsets your mom. In contrast, your dad often tells you that he would be happy if your mother remarried. From all of this you conclude that it was your dad who wanted out of the marriage and your mom who has suffered most. But there's a strong possibility that you're wrong. Not only are women *more* likely than men to get divorced because they have fallen in love with another person, but they are almost as likely as men to commit adultery.[16,17] And whichever parent feels the guiltiest about the divorce tries the hardest to appear innocent and blameless in the children's eyes, acts friendlier to the ex-spouse, and takes longer to remarry or to create a joyful life.[3,32] Most people who commit adultery do not end up marrying the person with whom they cheated.[33] And even when the woman is the one who cheated or who wanted out of the marriage for other reasons, she is usually more upset when her ex-husband remarries than he is when she remarries.[4,45]

Even though it is not in the best interests of your relationship with your parent to blame him or her for the divorce, it *is* in your best interests to have ongoing, candid discussions about the mistakes that both of them feel they made in their marriage—including adultery. If you don't have these ongoing talks, you're likely to keep blaming one of them—*and you're likely to have similar problems in your own intimate relationships.* As a young child, your parents should not tell you any sexual details about their lives or badmouth each other in front of you. But even at a young age you should not be lied to or deceived about the reasons for the divorce. Either of your parents can explain the divorce to you in an honest way that makes sense to you even as a very young child. For example, "Because daddy drinks a lot, mommy can't live with him anymore" or "Because mommy's new friend Sam makes her happier than daddy does, we are getting a divorce." As you get older, your parents should both talk to you more candidly about what went wrong—and encourage you to get the other's viewpoint. Doing this isn't a way of punishing, blaming, or preventing old wounds from healing. Doing this is a way of preventing your relationship with each of them from being permanently damaged and increasing the chance that you won't repeat their mistakes. So if your parents have not allowed or encouraged you to have candid conversations about their marital mistakes, ask each of them to give you this gift now.

You also might stop searching for the "bad guys" and the "good guys" by looking at your own behavior since your parents divorced. You haven't always been the "good guy" either. If you're honest with yourself, there are certain things that you have said or done that hurt your relationship with your father. Use the next two quizzes to think about what you could have done better.

Mistakes: Yours and Your Father's

How do you think you and your father would answer the following questions?

What three things have you and your father done since the divorce that have hurt your relationship?
Me:
1. _____
2. _____
3. _____
Dad:
1. _____
2. _____
3. _____

What do you wish each of you had done instead?
Me:
1. _____
2. _____
3. _____
Dad:
1. _____
2. _____
3. _____

What are three things you and your father did that were good for your relationship after the divorce?
Me:
1. _____
2. _____
3. _____

Dad:

1. _____

2. _____

3. _____

Treating Dad Like a Second-Class Parent

Since your parents' divorce, how have you treated your father? In addressing these issues, use 0 to mean "never," 1 to mean "rarely," 2 to mean "usually," and 3 to mean "almost always."

____ I spent more time visiting mother than father.

____ I spent more holidays with mom than with dad.

____ I put more thought into the gifts I gave my mother than those I gave my dad.

____ I phoned my mother more often than I phoned my dad.

____ I did more to celebrate mom's birthday or Mother's Day than dad's birthday or Father's Day.

____ I planned my visits first with mom before letting dad know when I'd be "free" to see him.

____ I spent the most important part of the holidays with mom (the main Thanksgiving meal).

____ I invited my friends to my mother's house more than to dad's house.

____ I went to visit my mother *before* going to visit my father.

____ I allowed my mother to talk more about their marriage and divorce than I allowed my dad.

____ Your score (30 possible)

Reconnecting: Starting Over with Dad

Nothing is more heart breaking than daughters and fathers who have not spoken to each other in years as a result of things that happened after the parents' divorce. Without exception, every daughter tells me that the reason she hasn't contacted her father is because he no longer loves her or misses her. And she believes that this is why he hasn't contacted her. If this is how you feel, I'd like you to try to imagine a different version of the story you've been telling yourself. Explore these 10 questions with me while I share the most common answers that most other daughters give me:

1. What was your relationship like in the first year after your parents stopped living together? *Most common answer:* "Pretty good. We spent time together regularly."

2. When did things start to change, and what was going on between your parents at that time? *Most common answers:* "He and I gradually stopped seeing as much of each other" and "Things between him and mom were bad."

3. What things did you do that might possibly have given your dad the idea that you were losing interest in him or that you were mad at him? *Common answers:* "Sometimes I refused to go visit him." "I said some mean things to him." "I hung up on him." "I stopped doing anything for his birthday." "I didn't invite him to my graduation." "I changed my last name to my stepfather's name." "I didn't want to talk to him very long when he'd call." "I would tell him at the last minute that I wasn't going to see him because I wanted to go somewhere with my friends instead."

4. What evidence do you have for assuming that the reason he stopped contacting you is that he didn't love you anymore? *Common answers:* "He got remarried" and "He had another kid and obviously doesn't need me anymore."

5. Are you sure that you can't think of one single time he tried to contact you during all that time? *Common answers:* "Well, he did write to me once, but . . . ," "Yes, he did send me a birthday present, but . . . ," and "He called once or twice, but. . . ."

6. Can you think of any possible reason why he might not have contacted you other than not loving you? *Common answers:* "He didn't like having to interact with mom." "He was embarrassed by his affair, and he felt guilty around me." "The things I said to him made him feel unloved." "Mom remarried, so maybe dad thought I didn't need him anymore since I had a stepfather." "He was afraid I would reject him or get mad at him."

7. What are the worst things you can imagine happening if you contacted him? *Common answers:* "He would reject me." "He wouldn't respond at all." "My mother would be very hurt or angry at me." "He would say bad things about my mother." "He would tell me things I don't want to know about the divorce." "He would start grilling me about what was going on in my mother's life." "He would start bragging about his new family." "There would just be this awkward silence because neither of us would know what to say."

8. If I could guarantee that none of those things would happen, would you want to talk to your father? Answer *every* time: "Yes."

9. If the worst things actually did happen, would you feel worse than you do now? Answer *every* time: "No."

10. What would it take to get you to contact him? What would have to happen? *Common answers:* "If he was very sick" and "If somebody told me that he wanted me to contact him."

If you and your dad have been out of touch for months, or even years, I'm urging you to take the first step and contact him. To help you get up the courage, I'd like you to identify what your fears are by answering the questions in the following box. As you think about contacting him, keep asking yourself: What have I got to lose, and what have I got to gain? Would I be any worse off if my efforts were a complete waste of time?

What Are You Afraid of?

List everything that you fear might happen if you contacted your father or if you asked him the things you want to know about the divorce. Then rate how likely those things are to happen and how you would feel if they did happen.

My Fear	How Likely Is It to Happen?	How Painful Would It Be?
He would not want to see me.	Not very	Extremely
My mother would be very hurt.	Very	Not very
He would hang up on me.		
He would not answer my letter.		
He would get really mad.		
He would say bad things about mom.		
He'd bring up things I don't want to discuss.		
We wouldn't know what to say—silence.		
I might cry.		
He would tell me about his other kids.		
I might lose my temper.		
Others		

Now list all the good things that might happen.
1. We could have a relationship again.
2. _____
3. _____
4. _____

Emotional Blackmail

If you're like most of the daughters I talk to, one reason you're afraid to contact your father is because you think it will upset your mother or a sibling: "My mom would be crushed." "My sister would be furious." "It would make mom feel bad that after all she's done for me, I still want to see him." What you have to keep in mind is this: You and your father have a right to a relationship with each other—one that you create together without anyone else's input or approval. In Chapter 3 we discussed emotional blackmail—a powerful form of manipulation in which people threaten to punish us emotionally if we don't do what they want.[48] The blackmailer sulks, gets angry, acts depressed, gets sick, gives you the cold shoulder, threatens to stop loving you, or uses any technique they think might make you feel guilty or afraid. Because they know you so well, they know what so say to make you feel guilty or insecure. They use emotional warfare to get you to do what they want. For instance, when you tell your mother that you are going to contact your father, she might get that look that makes you feel so sorry for her or so guilty. Or when you tell your sister that you're going to invite your dad for the holidays, she says that she won't come if he's there. We've already discussed ways to respond to emotional blackmail. You also might try giving your blackmailers a copy of my "bill of rights."

Daughter-Father Bill of Rights

As your daughter I have a right to:

- Have a relationship with my father no matter how anyone else feels
- Make my own decisions about forgiving him
- Not be quizzed by anyone about what's going on in my father's life
- Not have anyone try to influence my relationship with my dad
- Not have anyone joke or say negative things to me about him
- Not be made to feel guilty, disloyal, or unkind for having a relationship with my father

What to Say?

Once you have decided that you want to reconnect or rebuild your relationship with your father, where do you start? What do you say?

The Letter

If you aren't comfortable phoning him, why not start with a letter or an e-mail? A written message has several advantages: You can calmly think about what you want to say and how you want to say it. And your father will have time to think about how he wants to respond. Below is a sample letter to give you an idea of how to start. No matter how you word your letter, let me urge you to follow these guidelines: (1) Make it clear that you want to renew your relationship—not to ask for money, not to vent your anger, and not to rehash the past. (2) Explain why you've been afraid to get in touch before now. (3) Reassure him that you only want to focus on your relationship with each other—not on anyone else. (4) Offer at least one specific suggestion for how the two of you might start getting to know each other again. (5) Don't go overboard being too wordy or too detailed (lots will come up later as you spend more time writing and talking, but the first letter is not the place or the time to bring up the big issues. On the other hand, if you feel like apologizing for anything, go right ahead). (6) Don't say anything negative about him or anyone else. (7) Put a recent picture of yourself in with the letter— and ask your father to send you one of him. Trust me here. Do this. Why? Because when you see a picture of him, you probably won't feel as angry, as frightened, or as nervous. The father you have been imagining as so powerful or as so domineering, overbearing, self-confident, uncaring, distant, and threatening often looks so gentle, relaxed, harmless, tired, ordinary, fragile— and so old. And in seeing a picture of you, he might be able to let go of any image of you as an angry, frightening, judgmental, rejecting child.

What to Talk About

Now you can use those questions for "Getting to Know One Another" from Chapter 4. If you haven't seen him in a long time, send some of these

The Letter—What to Say?

Dear Dad, It's taken me a long time to get up the nerve to write you. I guess I'm afraid that you won't answer or that you'll say you don't want to hear from me again. I don't know exactly how to start or what to say, except that I'd like us to be in touch again. I'm not needing anything like money, and nobody has put me up to writing this. I just want us to have a relationship again. I think I understand a lot of things better now, and I have a few things I want to apologize for. Could we maybe start to write or phone? I've enclosed a picture of me from a few months ago with a few of my friends. Would you send me one of you? Well, that's about it for now.

questions to your father. Better yet, send him a copy of the whole chapter. You might say something like: "I was just thinking that since we've got so much to catch up on, and since I don't really know where to start, these questions might give us some things we'd both like to talk about."

Forgiveness

Now is also the time to reread the sections of Chapter 4 about apologizing and forgiving. These two old sayings may gently guide you along the way: "Anger is never without a reason, but seldom a very good one" and "Write injuries in sand and kindness in marble."

Is It Worth It?

When daughters decide to contact their fathers or decide to talk openly about difficult issues having to do with the divorce, what happens? Is it worth it? Do their worst fears come true? Before I share some of their stories, let me point out several things about all the daughters whose comments are included here. *All* had told me that their relationship with their father was distant or nonexistent before they decided to contact him or to have these conversations about their relationship. *None* had spent any time *alone* with their fathers since their parents' divorce—usually 5 or 6 years. *All* their fathers told the daughters that they were nervous about getting together to talk so openly about difficult issues. *All* were overjoyed when their daughter contacted them after months or years of not having any contact. *All* the fathers agreed to answer whatever questions their daughters asked about the divorce or their father-daughter relationship. *All* the fathers and the daughters said that talking about these difficult topics for hours without anyone else around was one of the best experiences they had shared since the parents' divorce—even though there were tears, awkward moments, and painful memories.

If you have wanted to know more about your parents' marriage and divorce, these daughters' stories should encourage you.

Nita: "As we talked, he actually admitted that he should have worked harder at his marriage to my mother. With regret in his voice, he said the saddest part of his life was not being around us kids enough after the divorce. And he said that he wished he had been more personal and loving in communicating with me. I couldn't believe he was so honest and open. I never imagined he could be like this."

Amanda: "Problems in my family are never discussed or explained—just ignored. Now, 10 years after my parents' divorce, because of this talk with my dad, I learned all the missing pieces leading up to the breakup of our family. I left him feeling I'd finally found someone who loves me and who had been taken away from me."

If you've ever assumed that your father wasn't deeply hurt by the divorce, consider these daughters' stories.

Michele: "One of my father's comments cut straight to my heart. When we were discussing his dreams, he said that he wonders if he will ever marry again. The expressive look on his face and tone of his voice showed me how much the divorce had hurt him. I stopped feeling mad at him because I saw him as a man with a lonely heart."

Laura: "The best thing was at the end of our long talk dad gave a big sigh and said, 'I was really nervous. I've been carrying those questions you sent me in my briefcase for the last 2 months so that I could read them over and over. I was really scared to answer some of them. You have never let me talk about my side of the divorce until now, which means more than you'll ever know.'"

If you have had a hard time understanding why your father isn't friendlier to your mother, these stories might help you.

Mary: "Hearing my father's story made me uncomfortable because I've tried so hard to maintain a positive image of my mother. After much thought, I've decided that it's still possible for me to admire her even though I see that what he told me about her is true. I'm glad he told me the truth."

Roseanne: "We finally talked about why he's angry at mom for not sharing any of the financial burden for our college educations. Once I was willing to listen to him and to stop defending my mom, I understood why he feels it's unfair for him to be paying for everything. I actually ended up agreeing with him."

Joan: "After letting him talk, I realize that he had to give up half his wealth when they divorced. Especially since my mom remarried so soon, he feels that she's spending his money to enjoy her life with another man. Finally, I see his side, not just hers."

If you thought the reason your father didn't spend more time with you was because he lost interest in you, pay careful attention to what these daughters have to say.

Pam: "He said that the saddest experience of his life was losing me. He said it again and again. I had no idea what an impact I'd had on him. I realized that he and I have wanted the same thing from each other all these years. But we never talked enough to figure that out. After we talked about the divorce, I realized that there's more to it than him being the bad guy and mom the good guy."

Lynette: "It had been 5 years since I'd seen my dad. I never thought I would get any response if I tried to contact him. When I sent him the letter, he immediately e-mailed back. He actually called himself a failure regarding my sister and me. I have begun to think it was a mistake to take my stepfather's name. I now realize that this may have made my dad feel that he wasn't needed. I never really thought about how he may have been hurt by that. He said my contacting him was the best gift I had ever given him. I always had this vision of him as some opinionated, overbearing, stubborn tyrant. It has always been unthinkable to me that he might admit his failures. Now I know that he actually does care. I realize now that seeing mom constantly upset by him while I was growing up had a profound effect on the way I feel about him. Now I know I have to focus on my issues with him—not on hers. I'm constantly amazed at his willingness for contact with me."

Alexandra: "The picture he said was most meaningful to him was one I had no idea meant anything to him—a picture of us together when I was a little girl. When I asked him if I could have the picture to take back home with me, he wouldn't let me because he always keeps it hanging in his bedroom. That made me cry. This long talk with my father is the most wonderful thing we have shared in over a decade. As I drove back to my place, I had a feeling I've never had before after spending time with him: I felt that I was *leaving* home rather than *coming* home."

Epilogue

As you've seen throughout this book, embracing your father more fully is one of the most crucial choices you can make in your life regardless of your age. Instead of ignoring, excluding, judging, deceiving, or rejecting him, you choose to accept, welcome, include, and open yourself more honestly to him. By taking the initiative and by putting the ideas from this book into practice, you give yourself many gifts.

As you move away from blaming, criticizing, and jumping to negative conclusions about your father, you give yourself the gift of seeing him more fully, more realistically, and more empathetically. You benefit because whenever you get rid of some of the anger, disappointment, illusions, and unrealistic expectations you have about another person, you feel more relaxed and more peaceful—not just around that person but within yourself. It's not that the other person has changed; it's that you have learned how to change your perceptions and your reactions. As a result, you free yourself from being as upset, as disappointed, or as agitated as you used to be.

Learning how to communicate more effectively and to get to know your father beyond his role as a parent, you allow him to give you special gifts—not money, not objects, but emotional gifts. You're better able to find those lovable and valuable parts of this man that you haven't fully seen or fully appreciated before. You also give yourself the gift of being more genuine and more honest with the man who has known you longer than anyone else on earth. Spending more time alone with your father and talking with him about the meaningful and personal parts of your life, you allow him to know you more fully. In this way, you rid yourself of the guilt and uneasiness that come from being superficial, from pretending to be someone you're not, from keeping secrets, and from deceiving. What relief and pleasure there are in being yourself around the one man who will love you longer than any other male in your life.

Above all, you give yourself the pride and self-esteem that come from having reached out to your father in new ways. You choose to do the embracing rather than to sit silently, angrily, or passively waiting for your father to be in charge of your relationship or to make the first move as though you were a helpless, young child. Regardless of how your father responds to your new behavior, you can feel better about yourself because you know that you're behaving like a self-directed, mature woman—not like a confused, immature girl.

Remember the story I told you in the Introduction about the three thirsty daughters? The first daughter dies of thirst because she doesn't know which tools to use to haul the water from the well. The second daughter is so thirsty that she has a throbbing headache. But she feels that it's too inconvenient and too much effort to haul the water. She wants someone else to get it for her. Besides, she almost fell into a well once when she was a little girl, so she's afraid. The third daughter and her father are both dying of thirst. Unfortunately, they have both been injured. They can't bend their elbows. Still, they manage to get the water hauled out of the well. But the way the bucket is designed, they can't bend their heads far enough into it to get any water. Unable to bend their elbows, neither has a way to get the water into his or her own mouth. But if they lift the bucket up together with their unbending arms and tilt it toward each of their mouths, they can assist the other in drinking to their heart's delight.

It is my hope that you will use what I have written to develop new tools, to overcome many of your fears, to realize that *only you* can haul the water from the well, and then to quench your own thirst for a more fulfilling relationship with your father by lifting the water to your father's lips—despite the injuries that you both have experienced along the way.

References

CHAPTER 1

1. Pruett, K. *Fatherneed.* New York: Free Press, 1999.
2. Geiger, B. *Fathers as Primary Caregivers.* New York: Greenwood Press, 1996.
3. Allport, S. *A Natural History of Parenting.* New York: Harmony Books, 1997.
4. Eyer, D. *Mother-Infant Bonding: A Scientific Fiction.* New Haven, CT: Yale University Press, 1994.
5. Hays, S. *The Cultural Contradictions of Motherhood.* New Haven, CT: Yale University Press, 1996.
6. Hardy, S. *Mother Nature.* New York: Ballantine Books, 1999.
7. Levine, J., and Pitinsky, T. *Working Fathers.* Reading, MA: Addison Wesley, 1998.
8. Booth, A., and Crouter, A. *Men in Families.* Mahwah, NJ: Erlbaum, 1998.
9. Dowd, N. *Redefining Fatherhood.* New York: Harcourt, 2000.
10. Barnett, R., and Rivers, C. *She Works, He Works.* San Francisco: Harper, 1996.
11. Hoffman, L., and Youngblade, L. *Mothers at Work.* New York: Cambridge University Press, 1999.
12. Lamb, M. (ed.) *The Role of the Father in Child Development.* New York: Wiley, 1997.
13. Thurer, S. *The Myths of Motherhood.* Boston: Houghton Mifflin, 1994.
14. Parker, R. *Mother Love, Mother Hate.* New York: Basic Books, 1996.
15. Gilovich, T. *How We Know What Isn't So.* New York: Macmillan, 1991.
16. Nisbett, R., and Ross, L. *The Person and the Situation.* New York: McGraw-Hill, 1991.
17. Thompson, M., and Hermann, D. *Autobiographical Memory.* Mahwah, NJ: Erlbaum, 1998.
18. Wilson, T. *Strangers to Ourselves.* New York: Knopf, 2002.
19. McAdams, D. *The Stories We Live By.* New York: William Morrow, 1993.
20. Rosenwald, G., and Ochberg, R. *Storied Lives.* New Haven, CT: Yale University Press, 1992.
21. Block, J. *Family Myths.* New York: Simon & Schuster, 1996.
22. Schacter, D. *Searching for Memory.* New York: Basic Books, 1996.
23. Farrell, W. *Father and Child Reunion.* New York: Tarcher Putnam, 2001.
24. Gates, A. Men on TV. *New York Times,* April 9, 2000, pp. 2–9.
25. Harshaw, T. Children's Books. *New York Times Review of Books,* September 14, 1997, p. 30.
26. Masson, J. *Emperor's Embrace: Animal Families and Fatherhood.* New York: Pocket Books, 1999.
27. Phares, V. *Poppa Psychology.* Westport, CT: Praeger, 1999.
28. Daniels, C. (ed.). *Lost Fathers.* New York: St. Martin's Press, 1998.

29. Nielsen, L. *Adolescence: A Contemporary View,* 3d ed. Ft. Worth, TX: Harcourt Brace, 1996.
30. Simon, C. *Fatherless Women.* New York: Wiley, 2001.
31. Cook, M., and Styron, W. *Fathers and Daughters.* New York: Chronicle Books, 1994.
32. Gayles, G. *Father Songs.* Boston: Beacon Press, 1997.
33. Perchinske, M. *Commitment: Fatherhood in Black America.* Rolo, MO: University of Missouri Press, 1998.
34. Smith, G. *Fathers: A Celebration.* New York: St. Martin's Press, 2000.
35. Grambling, L. *Daddy Will Be There.* New York: Greenwillow Books, 1998.
36. Vigna, J. *I Live with Daddy.* New York: Albert Whitman, 1997.
37. Spinelli, E. *Night Shift Daddy.* New York: Hyperion, 2000.

CHAPTER 2

1. Mellan, O. *Money Harmony.* New York: Walker, 1995.
2. Hirschfield, T. *Business Dad.* Boston: Little, Brown, 2000.
3. Levine, J., and Pitinsky, T. *Working Fathers.* Reading, MA: Addison Wesley, 1998.
4. Griswold, R. *Fatherhood in America.* New York: Basic Books, 1993.
5. Willis, S., and Reid, J. *Life in the Middle.* San Diego: Academic Press, 1999.
6. Ryff, C., and Seltzer, M. *The Parental Experience in Midlife.* Chicago: University of Chicago Press, 1996.
7. Booth, A., and Crouter, A. (eds.). *Men in Families.* Mahwah, NJ: Erlbaum, 1998.
8. Farrell, W. *Father and Child Reunion.* New York: Tarcher Putnam, 2001.
9. Brayfield, A. Juggling jobs and kids. *Journal of Marriage and the Family* 57:321–332, 2003.
10. Casper, L., and O'Connell, M. Work, income, and fathers as child care providers. *Demography* 35:243–250, 1998.
11. Bonney, J., Kelley, M., and Levant, R. Fathers in dual-earner families. *Journal of Family Psychology* 13:401–415, 1999.
12. Barnett, R., and Rivers, C. *She Works, He Works.* San Francisco: Harper, 1996.
13. Peters, J. *When Mothers Work.* Reading, MA: Addison Wesley, 1998.
14. Lamb, M. (ed.) *The Role of the Father in Child Development.* New York: Wiley, 1997.
15. Hoffman, L., and Youngblade, L. *Mothers at Work.* New York: Cambridge University Press, 1999.
16. Easthope, A. *What a Man's Gotta Do.* New York: Routledge, 1995.
17. Faludi, S. *Stiffed: The Betrayal of the American Man.* New York: William Morrow, 1999.
18. Spragins, E. When the Big Paycheck Is Hers. *New York Times,* January 6, 2002, p. BU-8.
19. Farrell, W. *Women Can't Hear What Men Don't Say.* New York: Tarcher Putnam, 2000.
20. Bellafante, G. My Big Fat Palace Wedding. *New York Times,* 2002, Sec. 9, p. 2
21. Frank, R. *Luxury Fever.* Princeton, NJ: Princeton University Press, 1999.
22. Klainer, P. *How Much Is Enough?* New York: Basic Books, 2000.
23. Schor, J. *The Overspent American.* New York: Basic Books, 1998.
24. Duguay, D. *Please Send Money.* New York: Perrenial, 2002.
25. Kravetz, S. *Welcome to the Real World.* New York: Norton, 1997.
26. Robbin, A., and Wilner, A. *Quarterlife Crisis.* Los Angeles: Tarcher, 2001.
27. Gold, D. Moneyed Young America. *New York Times,* October 11, 1998, p. 6.
28. Arnett, J. *Adolescence and Emerging Adulthood.* Englewood Cliffs, NJ: Prentice Hall, 2001.

29. Marino, V. The $249,180 Childhood. *New York Times,* February 9, 2003, p. 10.
30. Putzel, C. *Representing the Older Client in Divorce.* New York: Random House, 2000.
31. Mintz, S.From patriarchy to androgyny and other myths. In Booth, A. and Crouter, A. (eds.). *Men in Families.* Mahwah, NJ: Erlbaum, (1998), pp. 3-30.
32. Spragins, E. Loans from Parents. *New York Times,* March 3, 2002, p. 14.
33. Stanley, T., and Anko, W. *The Millionaire Next Door.* Atlanta: Longstreet Press, 1997.

CHAPTER 3

1. Goleman, D. *Emotional Intelligence.* New York: Bantam Books, 1995.
2. Pollack, W. *Real Boys.* New York: Henry Holt, 1999.
3. Bader, J. *He Meant, She Meant.* New York: Pantheon Books, 1999.
4. Farrell, W. *Women Can't Hear What Men Don't Say.* New York: Tarcher Putnam, 2000.
5. Chesler, P. *Woman's Inhumanity to Woman.* New York: Avalon Books, 2001.
6. Booth, A., and Crouter, A. (eds.). *Men in Families.* Mahwah, NJ: Erlbaum, 1998.
7. Kohn, A. *The Brighter Side of Human Nature: Altruism and Empathy.* New York: Basic Books, 1990.
8. Kindlon, D. T. M. *Raising Cain: Protecting the Emotional Life of Boys.* New York: Ballantine Books, 2000.
9. Levine, J., and Pitinsky, T. *Working Fathers.* Reading, MA: Addison Wesley, 1998.
10. Ryff, C., and Seltzer, M. *The Parental Experience in Midlife.* Chicago: University of Chicago Press, 1996.
11. Montemayor, R., McKenry, P., and Julian, T. The parental experience in mid life. In Shulman, S., and Collins, W. (eds.), *Father-Adolescent Relationships.* San Francisco: Jossey Bass, 1993, pp. 15-35.
12. Forward, S. *Emotional Blackmail.* New York: Harper Perrenial, 1998.
13. Tannen, D. *I Only Say This Because I Love You.* New York: Random House, 2001.
14. Patterson, K., Grenny, J., McMillan, R., and Switzler, A. *Crucial Conversations.* New York: McGraw-Hill, 2002.
15. Lamb, M. (ed.) *The Role of the Father in Child Development.* New York: Wiley, 1997.
16. Parke, R., and Brott, A. *Fatherhood.* Boston: Houghton Mifflin, 1999.
17. Pruett, K. *Fatherneed.* Boston: Free Press, 1999.
18. Snarey, J. *How Fathers Care for the Next Generation.* Cambridge, MA: Harvard University Press, 1993.
19. Nielsen, L. *Adolescence: A Contemporary View,* 3d ed. Ft. Worth, TX: Harcourt Brace, 1996.
20. Andersen, P. *Nonverbal Communication.* Los Angeles: Mayfield, 1998.

CHAPTER 4

1. Amato, P., and Booth, A. *Generation at Risk.* Cambridge, MA: Harvard University Press, 1997.
2. Apter, T. Fathers' closeness to teenage daughters. In Josselson, R., and Lieblich, A. (eds.), *The Narrative Study of Lives.* Newbury Park, CA: Sage, 1993, pp. 36–59.
3. Phares, V. *Poppa Psychology.* Westport, CT: Praeger, 1999.
4. Barnett, R. Adult daughter-parent relationships. *Journal of Marriage and the Family* 53:29–42, 1991.
5. Nielsen, L. Fathers and daughters: Why a course for college students? *College Student Journal* 35:280–317, 2001.

6. Rossi, A., and Rossi, P. *Of Human Bonding: Parent-Child Relations Across the Life Course.* New York: Aldine de Gruyter, 1990.
7. Aijan, D. *The Day My Father Died.* Philadelphia: Running Press, 1994.
8. Gayles, G. *Father Songs.* Boston: Beacon Press, 1997.
9. Owen, U. *Fathers: Reflections by Daughters.* New York: Pantheon Books, 1985.
10. Lamb, M. (ed.) *The Role of the Father in Child Development.* New York: Wiley, 1997.
11. Daniels, C. (ed.) *Lost Fathers.* New York: St. Martin's Press, 1998.
12. Griswold, R. *Fatherhood in America.* New York: Basic Books. (1993)
13. Mintz, S. From patriarchy to androgyny and other myths. In Booth, A., and Crouter, A. (eds.), *Men in Families.* Mahwah, NJ: Erlbaum, (1998), pp. 3-30.
14. . Nielsen, L. Fathers and daughters: Why a course for college students? *College Student Journal* 35: 280–317, 2001.
15. Nielsen, L. *Adolescence: A Contemporary View,* 3d ed. Ft. Worth, TX: Harcourt Brace, 1996.
16. Farrell, W. *Father and Child Reunion.* New York: Tarcher Putnam, 2001.
17. Heintz, K. *Family Issues on TV.* Washington, DC: National Partnership for Women and Families, 1998
18. Lupton, D., and Barclay, L. *Constructing Fatherhood.* Riverside, CA: Sage, 1997.
19. National Fatherhood Initiative. Fatherhood and television. *Fatherhood Today,* vol 1, p. 1, 2000.
20. Corneau, G. *Absent Fathers, Lost Sons.* Boston: Shambala, 1991.
21. Keyes, R. *Sons and Fathers.* New York: HarperCollins, 1992.
22. Pittman, F. *Man Enough: Fathers, Sons and the Search for Masculinity.* New York: Putnam, 1993.
23. Bloomfield, H. *Making Peace with Your Past.* New York: HarperCollins, 2000.
24. Engel, B. *Power of Apology.* New York: Wiley, 2001.
25. Safer, J. *Forgiving and Not Forgiving.* New York: Avon Books, 2000.
26. Powell, J. *Things I Should Have Said to My Father.* New York: Avon Books, 1994.
27. Garrod, A. *Emerging Themes in Moral Development.* Albany, NY: Teachers College Press, 1993.
28. Kurtines, W., and Gewirtz, J. *The Moral Development of Forgiveness.* Hillsdale, NJ: Erlbaum, 1992.
29. Kohn, A. *The Brighter Side of Human Nature: Altruism and Empathy.* New York: Basic Books, 1990.

CHAPTER 5

1. Lisle, D. *Without Child.* New York: Ballantine Books, 1996.
2. Lamb, M. (ed.) *The Role of the Father in Child Development.* New York: Wiley, 1997.
3. Nielsen, L. Fathers and daughters: Why a course for college students? *College Student Journal* 35:280–317, 2001.
4. Rossi, A., and Rossi, P. *Of Human Bonding.* New York: Aldine de Gruyter, 1990.
5. Bell-Scott, P. *Double Stitch.* New York: Harper Perennial, 1991.
6. Minuchin, S., and Nichols, M. *Family Healing.* New York: Simon & Schuster, 1994.
7. Karen, R. *Becoming Attached.* New York: Time Warner Books, 1994
8. Main, M. *Human Attachment.* New York: Cambridge University Press, 1993.
9. Cowan, C., and Cowan, P. *When Partners Become Parents.* Mahwah, NJ: Erlbaum, 2000.
10. Barnett, R., and Rivers, C. *She Works, He Works.* San Francisco: Harper, 1996.
11. Crosbie-Burnett, M., and Lewis. E. African American family structure. *Family Relations* 42:243–248, 1993.

12. Dadds, M. *Families, Children, and Development of Dysfunction.* Thousand Oaks, CA: Sage, 1994.
13. Booth, A., and Crouter, A. (eds.). *Men in Families.* Mahwah, NJ: Erlbaum, 1998.
14. Daniels, C. (ed.) *Lost Fathers.* New York: St. Martin's Press, 1998.
15. Dienhart, A. *Reshaping Fatherhood.* Thousand Oaks, CA: Sage, 1998.
16. Ellestad, J., and Stets, J. Jealousy and parenting. *Sociological Perspectives* 41:639–668, 1998.
17. Kammer, J. *Good Will Toward Men.* New York: St. Martin's Press, 1998.
18. Bowlby, J. *A Secure Base.* New York: Basic Books, 1988.
19. Miller, A. *Drama of the Gifted Child.* New York: Basic Books, 1994.
20. Dowd, N. *Redefining Fatherhood.* New York: Harcourt, 2000.
21. Parke, R., and Brott, A. *Fatherhood.* Boston: Houghton Mifflin, 1999.
22. Hinde, R., and Stevenson, J. *Relationships Within Families.* New York: Oxford University Press, 1995.
23. Parker, R. *Mother Love, Mother Hate.* New York: Basic Books, 1996.
24. Jacobvitz, D., and Bush, N. Parent-child alliances. *Developmental Psychology* 32:732–743, 1996.
25. Block, J. *Family Myths.* New York: Simon and Schuster, 1996.
26. Kitson, G., and Holmes, W. *Portrait of Divorce.* New York: Guilford, 1992.
27. Heyn, D. *Erotic Silence of the American Wife.* New York: Plume, 1997.
28. Adler, J. Adultery. *Newsweek,* September 30, 1996, pp. 54–60.
29. Roiphe, K. Adultery's Double Standard. *New York Times Magazine,* October 12, 1997, pp. 54–55.

CHAPTER 6

1. Reumann, M. *American Sexual Character* Berkeley: University of California Press, 2003.
2. Alan Guttmacher Institute. *Sex and America's Teenagers.* New York: Alan Guttmacher Institute, 2001.
3. Nielsen, L. *Adolescence: A Contemporary View,* 3d ed. Ft. Worth, TX: Harcourt Brace, 1996.
4. Thompson, S. *Going All the Way.* New York: Hill & Wang, 1995.
5. Kamen, P. *Her Way.* New York: New York University Press, 2001.
6. Holland, D., and Eisenhart, M. *Educated in Romance.* Chicago: University of Chicago Press, 1991.
7. Smith, L. *Becoming a Woman Through Romance.* New York: Routledge, 1990.
8. Vaux, R. *Ancient Israel.* New York: McGraw-Hill, 1960.
9. Broyard, B. *My Father Dancing: Stories.* New York: Knopf, (1999).
10. Owens, U. (ed.) *Fathers: Reflections by Daughters* New York: Pantheon, 1985.
11. Morgan, J. (ed.) *Fathers and Daughter: Memoirs and Stories.* New York: Signet, 2000.
12. Eicher, T. and Geller, J. (eds.) *Fathers and Daughters: Portraits in Fiction.* New York: Plume, 1990.

CHAPTER 7

1. U.S. Census Bureau. *Child Support to Custodial Parents.* Washington: U.S. Government Printing Office, 2003.
2. Ahrons, C. *The Good Divorce.* New York: HarperCollins, 1998.
3. Emery, R. *Marriage, Divorce, and Children's Adjustment.* Thousand Oaks, CA: Sage, 1999.

4. Hetherington, M. *For Better or Worse.* New York: Norton, 2003.
5. Krantzler, M., and Krantzler, P. *Moving Beyond Your Parents Divorce.* New York: McGraw-Hill, 2003.
6. Furstenberg, F., and Cherlin, A. *Divided Families.* Cambridge, MA: Harvard University Press, 1991.
7. Mason, M. *Custody Wars.* New York: Basic Books, 1999.
8. Schepard, A. *Children, Courts, and Custody.* New York: Cambridge University Press, 2003.
9. Guidibaldi, J., and Kuhn, R. Joint custody and divorce. *Speak Out For Children* Winter:8, 1998.
10. Baker, R., and Mcmurray, A. Fathers' loss of school involvement. *Journal of Family Issues* 3:201–214, 1998.
11. Carr, A. Including fathers in family therapy. *Contemporary Family Therapy* 20:371–383, 1998.
12. Long, N. Are we contributing to the devaluation of fathers? *Clinical Child Psychology and Psychiatry* 2:197–200, 1997.
13. Pruett, K. *Fatherneed.* Boston: Free Press, 1999.
14. Braver, S. *Divorced Dads.* New York: Putnam, 1999.
15. Farrell, W. *Father and Child Reunion.* New York: Tarcher Putnam, 2001.
16. Botwin, C. *Tempted Women: Female Infidelity.* Boston: Little, Brown, 1994.
17. Heyn, D. *Erotic Silence of the American Wife.* New York: Plume, 1997.
18. Gottman, J. *Seven Principles for Making Marriage Work.* Hillsdale, NJ: Crown, 1999.
19. Garfinkel, I. *Fathers under Fire: The Revolution in Child Support.* Belmont, CA: Sage, 1999.
20. Brott, A. *Single Father.* New York: Abbeville Press, 1999.
21. Greif, G. *Out of Touch.* New York: Oxford University Press, 1997.
22. Weitzman, L. *The Divorce Revolution.* Boston: Free Press, 1985.
23. Duncan, G., and Hoffman, S. Economic consequences of divorce. In David, M. (ed.), *Horizontal Equity and Economic Well-Being.* Chicago: University of Chicago Press, 1985 pp. 101-125.
24. Smock, P., Manning, W., and Gupta, S. Effect of marriage and divorce on women's economic well-being. *American Sociological Review* 64:794–812, 1999.
25. Bianchi, S., Subaiya, L., and Kahn, J. The gender gap in economic well-being of non-resident fathers and custodial mothers. *Demography* 36:195–203, 1999.
26. Putzel, C. *Representing the Older Client in Divorce.* New York: Random House, 2000.
27. Woodhouse, V. *Divorce and Money.* New York: Nolo Press, 2002
28. Arendell, T. *Fathers and Divorce.* Thousand Oaks, CA: Sage, 1995.
29. Bryan, M. *Prodigal Father.* New York: Three Rivers Press, 1997.
30. Warshak, R. *Divorce Poison.* New York: Regan Books, 2002.
31. Crosbie-Burnett, M., and Lewis, E. African-American family structure. *Family Relations* 42:243–248, 1993.
32. Guttman, J. *Divorce in Psychosocial Perspective.* Hillsdale, NJ: Erlbaum, 1993.
33. Kitson, G., and Holmes, W. *Portrait of Divorce.* New York: Guilford, 1992.
34. Ainsworth, M., and Eichberg, C. Mother's loss of attachment figure. In Parkes, C., Hinde, J., and Marris, P. (eds.), *Attachment Across the Life Cycle.* New York: Routledge, 1991, pp. 160–183.
35. Miller, A. *Drama of the Gifted Child.* New York: Basic Books, 1994.
36. Main, M. *Human Attachment.* Cambridge, England: Cambridge University Press, 1993.

37. Bernstein, A. Stepparents in movie plot summaries. *Marriage and Family Review* **26**:153–175, 1997.
38. Daly, M., and Wilson, M. *The Truth About Cinderella.* New Haven, CT: Yale University Press, 1999.
39. Warner, M. *From the Beast to the Blonde: On Fairy Tales and Their Tellers.* New York: Farrar, Strause & Giroux, 1996.
40. Bray, J., and Kelly, J. *Stepfamilies.* New York: Broadway Books, 1998.
41. Ganong, L., and Coleman, M. *Remarried Family Relationships.* Beverly Hills, CA: Erlbaum, 1999.
42. Visher, E., and Visher, J. *Therapy with Stepfamilies.* New York: Brunner Mazel, 1996.
43. Thompson, R., and Amato, P. *The Postdivorce Family.* Thousand Oaks, CA: Sage, 1999.
44. Depner, C., and Bray, J. *Nonresidential Parenting.* Newbury Park, CA: Sage, 1993.
45. Kelly, S. *Second Wives, Second Lives.* New York: William Morrow, 2000.
46. Nielsen, L. Stepmothers: Why so much stress? *Journal of Divorce and Remarriage* **30**:115–148, 1999.
47. Gardner, R. *Parental Alienation Syndrome.* Cresskill, NJ: Creative Therapeutics, 1998.
48. Forward, S. *Emotional Blackmail.* New York: Harper Perrenial, 1998.

Bibliography

Ahrons, C. *The Good Divorce.* New York: HarperCollins, 1998.

Amato, P., and Booth, A. *Generation at Risk.* Cambridge, MA: Harvard University Press, 1997.

Arendell, T. *Fathers and Divorce.* Thousand Oaks, CA: Sage, 1995.

Bader, J. *He Meant, She Meant.* New York: Pantheon Books, 1999.

Barnett, R., and Rivers, C. *She Works, He Works.* San Francisco: Harper, 1996.

Bell-Scott, P. *Double Stitch.* New York: Harper Perennial, 1991.

Berry, C. and Barrington, L. *Daddies and Daughters.* New York: Fireside, 1999.

Block, J. *Family Myths.* New York: Simon & Schuster, 1996.

Bloomfield, H. *Making Peace with Your Past.* New York: HarperCollins, 2000.

Boose, L., and Flowers, B. (eds.). *Daughters and Fathers.* Baltimore: Johns Hopkins University Press, 1989.

Booth, A., and Crouter, A. (eds.). *Men in Families.* Mahwah, NJ: Erlbaum, 1998.

Bowlby, J. *A Secure Base.* New York: Basic Books, 1988.

Braver, S. *Divorced Dads.* New York: Putnam, 1999.

Bray, J., and Kelly, J. *Stepfamilies.* New York: Broadway Books, 1998.

Brott, A. *Single Father.* New York: Abbeville Press, 1999.

Broyard, B. *My Father, Dancing: Stories.* New York: Knopf, 1999.

Bryan, M. *Prodigal Father.* New York: Three Rivers Press, 1997.

Buchanan, C., Maccoby, E., and Dornbusch, S. *Adolescents after Divorce.* Cambridge, MA: Harvard University Press, 1997.

Chesler, P. *Woman's Inhumanity to Woman.* New York: Avalon, 2001.

Chethik, N. *Father Loss.* New York: Hyperion, 2001.

Cook, M., and Styron, W. *Fathers and Daughters.* New York: Chronicle Books, 1994.

Cowan, C., and Cowan, P. *When Partners Become Parents.* Mahwah, NJ: Erlbaum, 2000.

Daly, M., and Wilson, M. *The Truth About Cinderella.* New Haven, CT: Yale University Press, 1999.

Daniels, C. (ed.) *Lost Fathers.* New York: St. Martin's Press, 1998.

Depner, C., and Bray, J. *Nonresidential Parenting.* Newbury Park, CA: Sage, 1993.

Dienhart, A. *Reshaping Fatherhood.* Thousand Oaks, CA: Sage, 1998.

Dodson, J. *Faithful Travelers: A Father, a Daughter, a Fly Fishing Journey of the Heart.* Boston: Bantam (1999)

Dowd, N. *Redefining Fatherhood.* New York: Harcourt, 2000.

Duguay, D. *Please Send Money.* New York: Perrenial, 2002.

Easthope, A. *What a Man's Gotta Do.* New York: Routledge, 1995.

Eicher, T. and Geller, J. (eds). *Fathers and Daughters: Portraits in Fiction.* New York: Plume, 1990.

Emery, R. *Marriage, Divorce, and Children's Adjustment.* Thousand Oaks, CA: Sage, 1999.

Engel, B. *Power of Apology.* New York: Wiley, 2001.

Erickson, B. *Longing for Dad.* Deerfield Beach, FL: Health Communications, 1998.

Faludi, S. *Stiffed: The Betrayal of the American Man.* New York: William Morrow, 1999.

Farrell, W. *Father and Child Reunion.* New York: Tarcher Putnam, 2001.

Farrell, W. *Women Can't Hear What Men Don't Say.* New York: Jeremy Tarcher, 2000.

Forward, S. *Emotional Blackmail.* New York: Harper Perrenial, 1998.

Frank, R. *Luxury Fever.* Princeton, NJ: Princeton University Press, 1999.

Furstenberg, F., and Cherlin, A. *Divided Families.* Cambridge, MA: Harvard University Press, 1991.

Ganong, L., and Coleman, M. *Remarried Family Relationships.* Beverly Hills, CA: Erlbaum, 1999.

Gardner, R. *Parental Alienation Syndrome.* Cresskill, NJ: Creative Therapeutics, 1998.

Garfinkel, I. *Fathers Under Fire: Revolution in Child Support.* Belmont, CA: Sage, 1999.

Gayles, G. *Father Songs*. Boston: Beacon Press, 1997.

Geiger, B. *Fathers as Primary Caregivers*. New York: Greenwood Press, 1996.

Godwin, G. *Father Melancholy's Daughter*. New York: William Morrow, 1991.

Goleman, D. *Emotional Intelligence*. New York: Bantam Books, 1995.

Goldberg, M. *The Bee Season*. New York: Anchor, 2001.

Gottman, J. *Seven Principles for Making Marriage Work*. Hillsdale, NJ: Crown, 1999.

Goulter, B., and Minninger, J. *The Father-Daughter Dance*. New York: Putnam, 1993.

Greif, G. *Out of Touch*. New York: Oxford University Press, 1997.

Griswold, R. *Fatherhood in America*. New York: Basic Books, 1993.

Guttman, J. *Divorce in Psychosocial Perspective*. Hillsdale, NJ: Erlbaum, 1993.

Hardy, S. *Mother Nature*. New York: Ballantine Books, 1999.

Harris, M. *The Loss That Is Forever*. New York: Plume, 1995.

Henry, D., and McPherson, J. (eds.) *Fathering Daughters: Reflections by Men* Boston: Beacon Press, 1998.

Hetherington, M. *For Better or Worse*. New York: Norton, 2003.

Heyn, D. *Erotic Silence of the American Wife*. New York: Plume, 1997.

Hinde, R., and Stevenson, J. (eds.). *Relationships in Families*. New York: Oxford University Press, 1995.

Hirschfield, T. *Business Dad*. Boston: Little, Brown, 2000.

Hoffman, L., and Youngblade, L. *Mothers at Work*. New York: Cambridge University Press, 1999.

Kammer, J. *Good Will Toward Men*. New York: St. Martin's Press, 1998.

Karen, R. *Becoming Attached*. New York: Time Warner Books, 1994.

Kast, V. *Father-Daughter, Mother-Son*. Rockport, MA: Element Press, 1997.

Kelly, J. *Fathers and Daughters*. New York: Broadway Books, 2002.

Kelly, S. *Second Wives, Second Lives*. New York: William Morrow, 2000.

Kitson, G., and Holmes, W. *Portrait of Divorce*. New York: Guilford, 1992.

Klainer, P. *How Much Is Enough?* New York: Basic Books, 2000.

Krantzler, M., and Krantzler, P. *Moving Beyond Your Parents' Divorce*. New York: McGraw-Hill, 2003.

Kravetz, S. *Welcome to the Real World*. New York: Norton, 1997.

Lamb, M. (ed.). *The Role of the Father in Child Development*. New York: Wiley, 1997.

Leonard, L. *The Wounded Woman: Healing the Father-Daughter Wound.* Boston: Shambala, 1998.

Levine, J., and Pitinsky, T. *Working Fathers.* Reading, MA: Addison Wesley, 1998.

Lupton, D., and Barclay, L. *Constructing Fatherhood.* Riverside, CA: Sage, 1997.

Main, M. *Human Attachment.* Cambridge, England: Cambridge University Press, 1993.

Maine, M. *Father Hunger.* New York: Gurze Books, 1991.

Mason, M. *Custody Wars.* New York: Basic Books, 1999.

Masson, J. *Emperor's Embrace: Animal Families and Fatherhood.* New York: Pocket Books, 1999.

McAdams, D. *The Stories We Live By.* New York: William Morrow, 1993.

McLanahan, S., and Sandefur, G. *Growing Up with a Single Parent.* Cambridge, MA: Harvard University Press, 1994.

Miller, A. *Drama of the Gifted Child.* New York: Basic Books, 1994.

Minuchin, S., and Nichols, M. *Family Healing.* New York: Simon & Schuster, 1994.

Morgan, J. (ed.). *Fathers and Daughters: Memoirs and Stories.* New York: Signet, 2000.

Murdock, M. *Fathers' Daughters.* New York: Fawcett, 1996.

Nielsen, L. *Adolescence: A Contemporary View.* Ft. Worth, TX: Harcourt Brace, 1996.

Norman, G. *Two For the Summit: My Daughter, the Mountain, and Me.* New York: Dutton, 2000.

Olds, S. *The Father.* New York: Random House, 1992.

Osherson, S. *The Passions of Fatherhood.* New York: Ballantine Books, 1995.

Owen, U. (ed.). *Fathers: Reflections by Daughters.* New York: Pantheon Books, 1985.

Parke, R., and Brott, A. *Fatherhood.* Boston: Houghton Mifflin, 1999.

Parker, R. *Mother Love, Mother Hate.* New York: Basic Books, 1996.

Pasley, K., and Ihinger-Tallman, M. (eds.). *Remarriage and Stepfamilies.* Westport, CT: Greenwood Press, 1994.

Patterson, K., Grenny, J., McMillan, R., and Switzler, A. *Crucial Conversations.* New York: McGraw-Hill, 2002.

Perchinske, M. *Commitment: Fatherhood in Black America.* Rolo, MO: University of Missouri Press, 1998.

Phares, V. *Poppa Psychology.* Westport, CT: Praeger, 1999.

Pollack, W. *Real Boys.* New York: Owl Books, 2000.

Popenoe, D. *Life Without Father.* Cambridge, MA: Harvard University Press, 1999.

Powell, J. *Things I Should Have Said to My Father.* New York: Avon Books, 1994.

Pruett, K. *Fatherneed.* New York: Free Press, 1999.

Putzel, C. *Representing the Older Client in Divorce.* New York: Random House, 2000.

Ricci, I. *Mom's House, Dad's House.* New York: Fireside Books, 1997.

Robbin, A., and Wilner, A. *Quarterlife Crisis.* Los Angeles: Tarcher, 2001.

Rosenwald, G., and Ochberg, R. *Storied Lives.* New Haven, CT: Yale University Press, 1992.

Rossi, A., and Rossi, P. *Of Human Bonding: Parent-Child Relations Across the Life Course.* New York: Aldine de Gruyter, 1990.

Ryff, C., and Seltzer, M. *The Parental Experience in Midlife.* Chicago: University of Chicago Press, 1996.

Safer, J. *Forgiving and Not Forgiving.* New York: Basic Books, 1996.

Schacter, D. *Searching for Memory.* New York: Basic Books, 1996.

Schor, J. *The Overspent American.* New York: Basic Books, 1998.

Scull, C. (ed.). *Fathers, Sons and Daughters.* Los Angeles: Tarcher, 1992.

Secunda, V. *Women and Their Fathers.* New York: Delacorte, 1992.

Sharpe, S. *Fathers and Daughters.* New York: Routledge, 1994.

Sheldon, B. *Daughters and Fathers in Feminist Novels.* Berlin: Peter Lang, 1997.

Shepard, A. *Children, Courts and Custody.* New York: Cambridge University Press, 2003.

Shulman, S., and Krenke, I. *Fathers and Adolescents.* New York: Routledge, 1996.

Simon, C. *Fatherless Women.* New York: Wiley, 2001.

Smith, G. *Fathers: A Celebration.* New York: St. Martin's Press, 2000.

Snarey, J. *How Fathers Care for the Next Generation.* Cambridge, MA: Harvard University Press, 1993.

Stein, J. *Fiddler on the Roof.* New York: Pocket Books, 1966.

Stone, G. *Fathering at Risk.* New York: Springer, 2001.

Sullivan, C. *Fathers and Children in Literature and Art.* New York: Harry Abrams, 1995.

Tannen, D. *I Only Say This Because I Love You.* New York: Random House, 2001.

Thompson, A., and Amato, P. (eds.). *The Postdivorce Family.* Thousand Oaks, CA: Sage, 1999.

Thurer, S. *The Myths of Motherhood.* Boston: Houghton Mifflin, 1994.

Twaite, J. *Children of Divorce.* New York: Jason Aronson, 1998.

U.S. Census Bureau. *U.S. Population: Selected Characteristics.* Washington: U.S. Government Printing Office, 2000.

Visher, E., and Visher, J. *Therapy with Stepfamilies.* New York: Brunner Mazel, 1996.

Wakerman, E. *Father Loss: Daughters Discuss the Man That Got Away.* New York: Henry Holt, 1984.

Wallerstein, J. *What About the Kids?* New York: Hyperion, 2003.

Warner, M. *From Beast to Blonde: Fairy Tales and Their Tellers.* New York: Farrar, Strause & Giroux, 1996.

Warshak, R. *Divorce Poison.* New York: Regan Books, 2002.

Wild, J. *Women, Men, and Children Surviving Divorce.* New York: Wiley, 2000.

Woodhouse, V. *Divorce and Money.* New York: Nolo Press, 2002.

Woodman, M. *Leaving My Father's House* Boston: Shambala,1992.

Zwinger, L. *Daughters, Fathers, and the Novel.* Madison: University of Wisconsin, 1991.

Index

About the Author

Dr. Linda Nielsen is a professor at Wake Forest University and author of the acclaimed 700-page textbook *Adolescence: A Contemporary View*. She also wrote a book for parents and teachers, *Motivating Adolescents*. Having worked with adolescent and young adult daughters for over 30 years, for the past 10 years she has been teaching the only course in the country devoted exclusively to father-daughter relationships. In her *Fathers and Daughters* course she has helped hundreds of young women strengthen or reestablish their relationships with their fathers. As a psychologist she has written numerous articles about adolescents and father-daughter relationships, devoting special attention to divorced fathers. The recipient of several awards for her research and writing, she lectures, presents seminars, appears on television, and offers assistance to fathers, daughters, and therapists across the country through her Web site and e-mails.